中国文化英语说

Talk about Chinese Culture in English

主　编　於芳

副主编　任吉丹　高森凤

浙江工商大学出版社
ZHEJIANG GONGSHANG UNIVERSITY PRESS

·杭州·

图书在版编目(CIP)数据

中国文化英语说 = Talk about Chinese Culture in English / 於芳主编. —杭州:浙江工商大学出版社, 2021.12(2022.8.1重印)

ISBN 978-7-5178-4739-7

Ⅰ.①中… Ⅱ.①於… Ⅲ.①英语课—中等专业学校—教材 Ⅳ.①G634.411

中国版本图书馆 CIP 数据核字(2021)第239635号

中国文化英语说 Talk about Chinese Culture in English
ZHONGGUO WENHUA YINGYU SHUO
於 芳 主编

责任编辑　杨　戈
封面设计　王亚英
责任印制　包建辉
出版发行　浙江工商大学出版社
　　　　　(杭州市教工路198号　邮政编码310012)
　　　　　(E-mail:zjgsupress@163.com)
　　　　　(网址:http://www.zjgsupress.com)
　　　　　电话:0571-88904980,88831806(传真)
排　　版　杭州朝曦图文设计有限公司
印　　刷　杭州宏雅印刷有限公司
开　　本　889mm×1194mm　1/16
印　　张　5.5
字　　数　140千
版 印 次　2021年12月第1版　2022年8月第2次印刷
书　　号　ISBN 978-7-5178-4739-7
定　　价　22.00元

前 言

中国人学英语,往往忽略中国文化的英语表达,学习者更注重通过了解英美文化培养英语思维能力,这就造成英语学习者能用英语流利表达英美文化而不能用英语交流中国文化的局面。2014年4月,教育部颁布的《关于全面深化课程改革 落实立德树人根本任务的意见》中提出了"核心素养"的概念,指出研制与构建核心素养体系是推进课程改革深化发展的关键。英语学科核心素养体系包括语言能力、文化品格、思维品质和学习能力。素养的构建对培养学生的国际意识和跨文化交际的能力具有十分重要的意义。英语学科核心素养的构建可以通过英语学科教学来实现。本书作为发展语言应用能力和提高文化素养的中等职业学校英语选修课教材,引入中华文明的教学内涵,为中等职业学校的英语学习者提供真实、丰富的语篇,将"听""说""读""写""译"等技能训练综合于一体,努力提升其英语综合应用能力与文化素质和人文素养,激发他们的民族归属感和自豪感。

1. 教材内容近生活

本书主要包括四个章节,分别是民俗文化、饮食文化、节日文化和茶文化。第一章民俗文化包含五小节,分别是中国生肖、颜色文化、数字文化、剪纸艺术和功夫文化;第二章饮食文化包含五小节,分别是餐桌礼仪、中国名菜、名小吃、筷子文化和宫保鸡丁;第三章节日文化包括五小节,分别是节日综述、春节、元宵、端午和中秋;第四章茶文化包括五小节,分别是茶文化、茶趣事、绿茶种类、西湖龙井和常见茶具。

2. 章节编排含用意

教材每个小节分为五个部分,即"中文导读""十个必背""三句必学""一篇必读"和"轻松一刻"。小节基本是按照点、线、面的方式编写,先从词到句,再到文。这样的形式便于学生接受与掌握。小节内容将理论和实践结合,让学生既能够静下来读,也能动起来做。"中文导读"呈现与本节内容相关的文化知识,便于学生了解本小节的背景知识。"十个必背"部分为与本小节相关的单词,配有解析与例句。"三句必学"为本小节口语表达常用句子,要求学生朗读和翻译,能够以背诵等形式机械输出。"一篇必读"涵盖与该小节主题相关的文化交流内容,为学生开展文化交流提供输出材料。"轻松一刻"是结合该小节主题增添的课外内容,让学生在文章学习之后得以自主学习。

3. 教材创新传文化

每个章节选取贴近学生生活的话题。结合知识背景,通过多种形式的输入后,让学生了解文化的概念、特征与功能,了解中国文化的悠久历史、多元化和丰富性。通过对本书的学习,学生可以深入了解自己国家的文化,可以向他人介绍、传播自己国家的文化。本书的创新之处在于定位拓展学习,目的相对明确,保证学生明确学习目标;内容贴近生活,话题贴近学生,使学生具备知识背景;内容由浅入深,形式相对丰富,令学生强化基本技能;评价层级区分明确,考核相对灵活,促进学生参与评价环节。

4. 学习平台来助力

借助 UMU 学习平台,我们发布的本书配套学习资源含:教学大纲 1 份、教学设计 20 课、教学课件 20 课、微课视频 10 个、习题大闯关 20 课。其他的资源后续还将增加、上传。

UMU 学习平台可在电脑端或手机 APP 中登录,具体方法如下:

运用访问码"se0531"。 学生可以在 UMU 网页或 APP 中输入访问码,或在在浏览器里中输入"https://pin.umu.cn",并输入访问码,登录学习。

由于编写组教师水平有限,如有疏漏,恳请各位专家、教师批评指正。

本书编者

2021 年 10 月

目　录

编委会名单

主　编:於　芳

副主编:任吉丹　高森凤

参　编:丁莉维　钱湘莺　吴培芳

Chapter 1

Folkways in Chinese Culture

1-1　中国生肖排一排 Chinese Zodiac

🕀 中文导读

十二生肖,又叫属相,包括鼠、牛、虎、兔、龙、蛇、马、羊、猴、鸡、狗、猪。十二生肖的起源与动物崇拜有关。据湖北云梦睡虎地和甘肃天水放马滩出土的秦简可知,先秦时期即有比较完整的生肖系统存在。最早记载与现代相同的十二生肖的传世文献是东汉王充的《论衡》。

十二生肖是十二地支的形象化代表,随着历史的发展,逐渐融入相生相克的民间信仰观念,表现在婚姻、人生、年运等方面。每一种生肖都有丰富的传说,并以此形成一种观念阐释系统,成为民间文化中的形象哲学,如婚配上的属相、庙会祈祷、本命年等。

⚛ 十个必背 The more you learn, the more you know.

1. **penguin** [ˈpeŋgwɪn] *n.* 企鹅

   There are all sorts of animals, including bears, pigs, kangaroos, and penguins.

   有各种各样的动物,包括熊、猪、袋鼠和企鹅。

2. **zodiacal** [zoʊˈdaɪəkl] *adj.* 黄道带的;星座的

   Capricorn is one of the most stable and serious of the zodiacal types.

   摩羯座是十二星座中最稳定和严肃的。

3. **cycle** [ˈsaɪkl] *n.* 周期;循环

   These tips will help you start a new cycle of sleep and wakefulness.

   这些小贴士将帮助你开启一个新的睡眠和清醒周期。

4. **calculate** [ˈkælkjuleit] *v.* 计算

   Their movements through the region were calculated to terrify landowners into abandoning their holdings.

   他们在该地区的行动是精心谋划的,意在恐吓土地所有者放弃手中的地产。

5. **lunar** [ˈluːnər] *adj.* 月球的;月亮的

   The lunar gravity is about one-sixth that on earth.

   月亮的引力大约为地球的六分之一。

6. **calendar** [ˈkælɪndə] *n.* 日历;挂历;日程表

   He marked off the days on a calendar.

   他标出日历上的日期。

7. **astrology** [əˈstrɑːlədʒi] *n.* 占星术;占星学;原始天文学

3

This discovery seems to validate the claims of popular astrology.

这个发现似乎能印证流行占星术的一些说法。

8. thoughtful [ˈθɔːtfl] *adj.* 周到的；体贴的

We provide customers with all-weather warm and thoughtful service.

我们为客户提供全天候热情周到的服务。

9. inspire [ɪnˈspaɪər] *vt.* 激励；鼓舞；赋予灵感

She has inspired a whole generation of fashion school graduates.

她激励了整整一届时装学校的毕业生。

10. stubborn [ˈstʌbərn] *adj.* 固执的；顽固的；倔强的；执拗的；难以去除（或对付）的

Her stubborn streak makes her very difficult to work with sometimes.

她固执的个性使得有时和她一起工作十分困难。

三句必学 The more you practice, the more fluently you will speak.

1. The Chinese Zodiac, known as Sheng Xiao, is based on a twelve-year **cycle**.
中国的生肖以12年为一个周期。

2. 2021 is the Year of the Ox starting from the Chinese New Year on February 12th in 2021 and lasting to Lunar New Year's Eve on January 31st in 2022.
2021年是牛年，从2021年2月12日的农历新年开始，持续到2022年1月31日的农历除夕。

3. People born in the Year of the Ox are often considered to be confident, patient, thoughtful and hardworking.
牛年出生的人常被认为是自信、耐心、体贴和勤奋的。

一篇必读 The more you read, the more knowledge you will get.

We can see many animals in the zoo, such as giraffes, elephants, **penguin**s, hippos and so on. What's more, we can also find different animals in some proverbs, such as "a rat in a hole", "as poor as a church mouse", "a paper tiger", "a snake in the grass", "eat like a horse", "make a monkey out of" and so on.

However, do you know 12 **zodiacal** animals in China? The Chinese Zodiac, known as Sheng Xiao, is based on a twelve-year **cycle**. Each year in the cycle is related to one animal sign. These animal signs are the rat, ox, tiger, rabbit, dragon, snake, horse, sheep, monkey, rooster, dog and pig in order. It is **calculated** according to Chinese **lunar calendar**.

2021 is the Year of the Ox, starting from the Chinese New Year on Feb.12 in 2021 and lasting to Lunar New Year's Eve on Jan. 31 in 2022. The animal year when a person was born is called his Ben Ming Nian (Zodiac Year of Birth). People will meet their birth signs once in every 12-year cycle. Chinese people take their year of birth seriously.

The 12 zodiacal animals symbolize different personal characteristics. According to Chinese **astrology**, people born in the Year of the Ox are often considered to be confident, patient, **thoughtful** and hardworking. They can **inspire** confidence in others. Born to lead, they can be quite **stubborn**.

1. Translate these phrases with animals.

（1）a rat in a hole

（2）as poor as a church mouse

（3）a paper tiger

（4）a snake in the grass

（5）eat like a horse

（6）make a monkey out of

2. Name the twelve zodiac animals in turn.

（1）_____ （2）_____ （3）_____ （4）_____ （5）_____ （6）_____

（7）_____ （8）_____ （9）_____ （10）_____ （11）_____ （12）_____

3. Complete your group's speech draft.

Topic：Chinese Zodiac

轻松一刻 **The more you share, the happier you will be.**

12 Zodiac Signs and Time

	Hours	Description
Rat	Zi Shi: 11 p.m. to 1 a.m.	This is the time rats actively **seek**（寻找）food.
Ox	Chou Shi: 1 to 3 a.m.	This is the time that oxen **ruminate**（沉思）.
Tiger	Yin Shi: 3 to 5 a.m.	Tigers hunt prey and **display**（显露）fiercest nature.
Rabbit	Mao Shi: 5 to 7 a.m.	The Jade Rabbit on the moon is busy pounding medicinal **herb**（药草）with a **pestle**（杵）.
Dragon	Chen Shi: 7 to 9 a.m.	Dragons are **hovering**（盘旋）in the sky at that time to give people rainfall.
Snake	Si Shi: 9 to 11 a.m.	Snakes start to leave their **burrows**（洞穴）.
Horse	Wu Shi: 11 a.m. to 1 p.m.	With the sun high above, other animals are lying down for a noon break while the horse is still **vigorous**（精力充沛的）.
Sheep	Wei Shi: 1 to 3 p.m.	It is said that if sheep ate grass at this time, they would grow stronger.
Monkey	Shen Shi: 3 to 5 p.m.	Monkeys become lively.
Rooster	You Shi: 5 to 7 p.m.	Roosters return to their **roost**（栖息处）as it is dark.
Dog	Xu Shi: 7 to 9 p.m.	Dogs begin to carry out their duty to guard entrances.
Pig	Hai Shi: 9 to 11 p.m.	All is quiet and pigs are sleeping soundly.

1-2 中国颜色辨一辨 Colors in Chinese Culture

中文导读

　　中国传统颜色五彩缤纷,色泽细腻,涵盖领域宽广且各色又分别表达不同的内涵和象征意义。扎根于中华文明沃土的色彩文化,无论是表现形式,还是应用规律,都被深深烙上了中国印记。色彩因中国文化的灿烂而愈加深邃,中国文化亦因色彩的绚丽而愈加多姿。色彩文化就在我们身边,也渗透在我们的血液中。中华民族的红色情结,儒、释、道的本色,文学艺术的创造,甚至那传承至今的民风民俗,无不投射出色彩文化的影子。

十个必背 The more you learn, the more you know.

1. symbol [ˈsɪmbl] *n.* 象征;符号;代号

White has always been a symbol of purity in Western cultures.

在西方文化中,白色一向象征纯洁。

2. envelope [ˈenvəloʊp] *n.* 信封;塑料封套;塑料封皮

I put "please forward" on the envelope.

我在信封上写了"请转递"。

3. occasion [əˈkeɪʒn] *n.* 场合;时机

Foreign visitors help to give a truly international flavor to the occasion.

外国客人使这个场合显出一种真正国际性的气氛。

4. association [əˌsoʊʃiˈeɪʃn] *n.* 协会;社团;联盟;联合;合伙;关联;交往;联想;联系

The association was formed to represent the interests of women artists.

成立这个协会是为了维护女性艺术家的利益。

5. rank [ræŋk] *v.* 排列;把……分等级;属于某等级;使排成行

Rank the states in the order of size.

按大小把这些州排列一下。

6. neutrality [nuːˈtræləti] *n.* 中立;中立状态

We have tried to pursue a policy of neutrality.

我们力行中立的政策。

7. attire [əˈtaɪər] *n.* 服装;衣服

Her attention was attracted by his peculiar attire.

他那奇特的服装引起了她的注意。

8. element [ˈelɪmənt] *n.* 要素;基本部分

Fitness has now become an important element in our lives.

现在健康已经成为我们生活中的一个要素。

9. harmony [ˈhɑːrməni] *n.* 和谐;协调;融洽,一致;[音] 和声

We must try to live in peace and harmony with ourselves and those around us.

我们必须努力和我们自己及周围的人和睦相处。

10. advocate [ˈædvəkeɪt] *vt.* 拥护;支持;提倡

Many experts advocate rewarding your child for good behavior.

很多专家主张对小孩的良好表现加以奖励。

三句必学 The more you practice, the more fluently you will speak.

1. Red is a **symbol** of good luck and happiness in Chinese culture.

   在中国文化中,红色是好运和幸福的象征。

2. Associated with but **rank**ed above brown, yellow signifies **neutrality** and good luck.

   黄色与棕色相关,但排名高于棕色,黄色象征中立和好运。

3. Green is related to recovery and growth and it is also a symbol of health and environmental protection.

   绿色与复苏和生长有关,也是健康和环境保护的象征。

一篇必读 The more you read, the more knowledge you will get.

In traditional Chinese art and culture, black, red, cyan(青), white and yellow are viewed as standard colors. These colors correspond to the five elements of water, fire, wood, metal and earth, taught in traditional Chinese physics. Each color in Chinese culture refers to the certain values that Chinese culture attaches to colors.

Element	Wood	Fire	Earth	Metal	Water
Color	Cyan	Red	Yellow	White	Black

Red

Red is a **symbol** of good luck and happiness in Chinese culture. We can find red everywhere during Chinese New Year and other holiday celebrations. Cash is usually put in red **envelopes** as gifts to relatives and friends during special **occasions**. Red is much-welcomed in China somewhat because of its **association** with Chinese revolutions and the Communist Party.

Yellow

Associated with but **rank**ed above brown, yellow signifies **neutrality** and good luck. Yellow was the emperor's color in Imperial China. Yellow often decorates royal palaces, altars and temples. The color was used in the robes and **attire** of the emperors. Yellow also represents freedom from worldly cares and thus it is used in Buddhism. The **element**s of Buddhist temples are yellow.

Green

Green means a lot. People impose a mean meaning on green, such as "a green look" or "a green hat". At the same time, people regard green as a symbol of **harmony**. It symbolizes balance and peace. Green is related to recovery and growth and it is also a symbol of health and environmental protection. Today's society has been **advocating** green chemistry, green vegetables and green food.

1. Fill in the blanks.

In traditional Chinese art and culture, _____, _____, _____, _____ and _____ are viewed as standard colors. These colors correspond to the five elements of _____, _____, _____, _____ and _____, taught in traditional Chinese physics.

2. Translate the following sentences.

（1）Red is a symbol of good luck and happiness in Chinese culture.

_____

（2）Yellow was the emperor's color in Imperial China.

_____

（3）People regard green as a symbol of harmony.

_____

3. Complete your group's speech draft.

Topic：Colors in Chinese culture

🐌 **轻松一刻 The more you share, the happier you will be.**

White & Black

White, **corresponding**（相关的）with metal, represents gold and symbolizes brightness, purity, and **fulfillment**（满足感）. White is also the color of **mourning**（哀悼）. It is associated with death and is used **predominantly**（多数情况下）in funerals in Chinese culture. Ancient Chinese people wore white clothes and hats only when they mourned for the dead.

Black, corresponding to water, is a **neutral**（中立的）color. *The I Ching*, or *Book of Changes*, regards black as Heaven's color. The Tai Ji symbol uses black and white to represent the unity of yin and yang. Ancient Chinese people regarded black as the king of colors and honored black more **consistently**（一贯地）than any other color. Lao Zi said that five colors make people blind, so the Dao School chose black as the color of the Dao.

1-3 中国数字认一认 Numbers in Chinese Culture

中文导读

从科学角度讲,数字的功能是计算。从文学和生活的角度讲,数字的功能是表义,数字经过"神化"计算后成为"玄数""虚数""天数"……在中国传统文化里,那些玄妙又神秘的数字又代表什么?

一元之数,万物开泰;两仪之数,混沌未开;

三才之数,天地人和;四象之数,待于生发;

五行之数,循环相生;七政之数,吉星照耀;

八卦之数,无穷无尽;大成之数,蕴含凶险。

十个必背 The more you learn, the more you know.

1. **superstitious** [ˌsuːpərˈstɪʃəs] *adj.* 迷信的;有迷信观念的

   Joan was extremely superstitious and believed the color green brought bad luck.

   琼十分迷信,她认为绿色不吉利。

2. **auspicious** [ɔˈspɪʃəs] *adj.* 吉利的;有前途的;有希望的;有利的

   His career as a playwright had an auspicious start.

   他的剧作家生涯有了一个好的开头。

3. **connote** [kəˈnoʊt] *v.* 隐含;暗示;意味着

   The term "organization" often connotes a sense of neatness.

   "organization"这个词常常让人想到整洁。

4. **stability** [stəˈbɪləti] *n.* 稳定性;稳定(性);稳固(性)

   Political stability, meanwhile, will be a prime concern.

   同时,政治稳定性将放在首位。

5. **multiply** [ˈmʌltɪplaɪ] *v.* 乘;乘以;成倍增加;迅速增加;(使)繁殖,增殖

   Our problems have multiplied since last year.

   自去年以来,我们的问题成倍增加。

6. **character** [ˈkærəktər] *n.* (事物、事件或地方的)特征

   Weeds are an index to the character of the soil.

   杂草是反映土壤特征的一个指标。

7. slick [slɪk] *adj.* 光滑的;华而不实的;熟练的,灵巧的;机灵的,聪明的

There's a big difference between an amateur video and a slick Hollywood production.

业余人士拍摄的视频片段和制作精良的好莱坞影片之间存在着巨大的差距。

8. fortune [ˈfɔːtʃən] *n.* 财富(尤指影响人生的)机会,运气;大笔的钱

His socialist views sit uneasily with his huge fortune.

他拥有大量财富,这与他的社会主义观点格格不入。

9. awesome [ˈɔːsəm] *adj.* 令人惊叹的

But this awesome person is too lifelike to be a god.

但这个令人惊叹的形象实在太真实、太鲜活。

10. embroider [ɪmˈbrɔɪdər] *v.* 刺绣;加以渲染(或润色);添枝加叶

She did beautiful needlework and she embroidered table napkins.

她的针线活很漂亮,并且她还会刺绣台布。

三句必学 The more you practice, the more fluently you will speak.

1. Some numbers are considered **auspicious**, while others the opposite or neutral.
有些数字被认为是吉祥的,而另一些则是相反的或中性的。

2. In the south of China, the pronunciation of 6 is similar to that of "fortune".
在中国南方,六的发音与"禄(财富)"相似。

3. It sounds the same as "久", meaning long-lasting.
这听起来和"久"发音相同,代表持久的意思。

一篇必读 The more you read, the more knowledge you will get.

Many people in China, if not all, are quite **superstitious** about numbers. Some numbers are considered **auspicious**, while others the opposite or neutral. Let's go through some numbers and see what they mean to the Chinese people.

The number 2 is regarded as a lucky number, as Chinese people like to say, "good things come in pairs (好事成双)." Thus, for events like weddings, people always like to choose dates with even numbers. This is because 2 **connotes** balance and **stability**. Ancient Chinese people believed that all things have two opposite yet connected aspects, such as yin and yang.

The number 3 is also a lucky one, for it represents "many" or means "to **multiply**". *Tao Te Ching*, an ancient Chinese book, explains how the world came into being: "Dao gives birth to one, one to two, two to three, and three to ten thousand things." In other words, three is a tipping point for multiplication. Since "人" means a person in Chinese, the **character** "众"(three people) means many people.

The number 6 is widely considered to be auspicious in the country. In the north of China, it sounds similar to "**slick**" or "smooth", so people are convinced that such a number will help to make things go smoothly. In the south of China, the pronunciation of 6 is similar to that of "**fortune**". Surely, it is quite lucky.

Recently, "666" is getting popular among young people, for whom this combination means "**awesome**".

The number 8 is always believed very auspicious, especially in the south of China. Its pronunciation is similar to "**prosper**". People in China often like to have this digit in their phone numbers, license plates, etc.

The number 9 is a lucky number as well. It sounds the same as "久", meaning long-lasting. An odd number is often associated with yang in a Chinese mind. Thus, as the biggest single digit, the top yang number 9 was often associated with emperors or imperials in ancient China. For instance, there is Nine-Dragon Screen in the Forbidden City. Meanwhile the emperors' official robes are **embroidered** with nine dragons.

1. Fill in the blanks.

The number 3 is a lucky one, too, for it represents "many" or means "to _____". *Tao Te Ching*, an _____ Chinese book, explains how the world _____ into being like this: "Dao gives _____ to one, one to two, two to three, and three to ten _____ things."

2. Translate the following sentences.

(1) In the north of China, it sounds similar to "slick" or "smooth", so people are convinced that such a number will help to make things go smoothly.

_____

(2) The number 8 is always believed very auspicious, especially in the south of China. Its pronunciation is similar to "prosper".

_____

(3) For instance, there is Nine-Dragon Screen in the Forbidden City. Meanwhile the emperors' official robes are **embroidered** with nine dragons.

_____

3. Complete your group's speech draft.

Topic: Numbers in Chinese Culture

轻松一刻 The more you share, the happier you will be.

In short, the pronunciation of numbers determines, to a large extent, whether a number is considered lucky or not. In modern days, young people in China still like to play with pronunciation of numbers and use those numbers to express their feelings.

Can you guess what they are trying to say with the following numbers?

1. 520（五二零）

2. 1314（一三一四）

1-4　中国剪纸剪一剪Chinese Paper-Cutting

中文导读

中国剪纸是一种用剪刀或刻刀在纸上剪刻花纹,用于装点生活或配合其他民俗活动的民间艺术。在中国,剪纸具有广泛的群众基础,融于各族人民的社会生活,是各种民俗活动的重要组成部分。其传神的造型和视觉形象,历经千年传承,蕴含了丰富的文化和历史信息,表达了广大民众的社会认知、道德观念、实践经验、生活理想和审美情趣,具有认知、教化、表意、抒情、娱乐、沟通等多重社会价值。

2006年5月20日,剪纸艺术经国务院批准列入第一批国家级非物质文化遗产名录。2009年9月28日至10月2日举行的联合国教科文组织保护非物质文化遗产政府间委员会第四次会议上,中国申报的中国剪纸项目入选"人类非物质文化遗产代表作名录"。

十个必背 The more you learn, the more you know.

1. critical [ˈkrɪtɪkəl] *adj.* 关键的;批评的,爱挑剔的;严重的;极重要的

The incident happened at a critical point in the campaign.

该事件发生在竞选活动的关键时期。

2. glue [glu] *v.* 胶合;紧附于

Glue the fabric around the window.

用胶水把布料粘在窗户周围。

3. symbolize [ˈsɪmbəˌlaɪz] *v.* 使用符号;采用象征;作为……的象征

They symbolize immortality and longevity.

它们象征着不朽和长寿。

4. elementary [ˌelɪˈmentri] *adj.* 初级的;基本的;基础的;简单的;容易的

The education in that school is elementary.

那所学校的教育是初级的。

5. square [skweə] *n.* (通常为方形的)广场;平方;正方形;四方形;正方形物;二次幂

He bent the wire into the shape of a square.

他把铁丝折成正方形。

6. fold [foʊld] *v.* 折叠;合拢;抱住;笼罩

He folded the paper carefully.

他把纸小心地折起来。

7. edge [ɛdʒ] *n.* 边;优势;(悬崖、峭壁的)边缘,端;锋利,尖锐

We were on a hill, right on the edge of town.

我们刚好位于城镇边缘的一座小山上。

8. rectangle [ˈrɛkˌtæŋgəl] *n.* [数]长方形,矩形

Suppose the width of a rectangle is *x* meters.

设长方形的宽是 *x* 米。

9. extend [ɪkˈstɛnd] *v.* 延长;伸展;给予;发出(邀请、欢迎等)

The caves extend for some 18 kilometers.

那些洞穴深约18千米。

10. accomplish [əˈkɑːmplɪʃ] *vt.* 完成

The first part of the plan has been safely accomplished.

计划的第一部分已顺利完成。

三句必学 The more you practice, the more fluently you will speak.

1. "囍" is an ancient Chinese word for happiness and it is also the most popular pattern used in the Chinese paper-cut art.

"囍"是一个表示幸福的古汉字,它也是中国剪纸艺术中最流行的图案。

2. You should have 7 **rectangles** in total—5 on one side and 2 on the other.

你应该总共有7个矩形——一边5个,另一边2个。

3. Now, post the paper on the window or door and introduce this wonderful piece to your friends!

现在,把剪纸贴在窗户或门上,并把这幅美妙的作品介绍给你的朋友!

一篇必读 The more you read, the more knowledge you will get.

Chinese paper-cut art is a **critical** cultural piece in China. It is used in all kinds of celebrations including wedding, promotion and moving to a new house. The paper art will be **glue**d on the door or window to **symbolize** happiness and good luck. "囍" is an ancient Chinese word for happiness and it is also the most popular pattern used in the Chinese paper-cut art.

Skill required: **Elementary** level—All ages can practice.

Time required: 5 minutes.

Let's start! Hope you will enjoy!

Step 1: Prepare your tool. Get ready with tools, which are a pencil, a pair of scissors, a piece of red **square** paper and a ruler.

Step 2: Fold the paper. Fold the paper two times. Now you will have a paper that is only fourth of the original size.

Step 3: Draw cutting lines. Draw two straight yellow lines. Turn the open **edge** side towards you and draw 5 rectangles with same sizes, another 2 rectangles in the other side. You should have 7 rectangles in total—5 on one side and 2 on the other.

Step 4: Cut the paper. Cut out the rectangles by following the yellow lines. Cut off all the 7 **rectangle**s carefully. Be care and make sure you cut the right lines. Otherwise, you will get a totally different pattern.

Step 5: Extend the pattern. After the cutting, the paper edges are sometimes sticking together. Be tender, when you extend it. Otherwise, you will tear it. You will see the final product with a very symmetric shape.

Step 6: Post it on windows. Congratulations! You **accomplished** the paper-cut art. Now, post the paper art on the window or door and introduce this wonderful piece to your friends!

1. Describe these shapes.

▭	●	▲	▭	★	─
正方形	圆形	三角形	长方形	五角星	直线

2. Translate the following sentences.

Step 1: Prepare your tool. _____

Step 2: Fold the paper. _____

Step 3: Draw cutting lines. _____

Step 4: Cut the paper. _____

Step 5: Extend the pattern. _____

Step 6: Post it on windows. _____

3. Complete your group's speech draft.

Topic：How to Make a Chinese Paper-Cut Art

轻松一刻 The more you share, the happier you will be.

China has the history of more than five thousand years. As a result, there are many traditional arts that have been inherited, such as paper-cutting. It is a kind of amazing art. People can use scissors to cut different shapes, like flowers and animals. When foreigners see the paper-cutting, they are surprised and give big applause to this great art.

How to be creative in the paper-cut art? The tricky part in this type of art is two things: Fold the paper how many times and cut the paper how complicated the pattern is. So if you can be creative in patterns and folding times, you will discover a much larger paper-cut art world.

Always remember "practice makes perfect". So pick up you scissors and have a go!

1-5 中国功夫练一练 Chinese Kungfu

中文导读

　　功夫,是中华民族智慧的结晶,是中华传统文化的体现,是世界上独一无二的"武化"。它讲究刚柔并济、内外兼修,既有刚健雄美的外形,更有典雅深邃的内涵,蕴含着先哲们对生命和宇宙的参悟,是中国劳动人民长期积累起来的宝贵文化遗产。

　　中国功夫在世界上影响广泛,不仅出现了大量中国功夫题材的中外影视作品,更有少林、太极、咏春拳等在全球广泛传扬。

十个必背 The more you learn, the more you know.

1. martial ['mɑ:ʃl] *adj.* 军事的;战争的;尚武的,好战的;战神玛尔斯的

The paper was actually twice banned under the martial regime.

在军政府时期,该报纸其实曾经两度遭禁。

2. utilize ['jutl,aɪz] *v.* 利用,使用

Sound engineers utilize a range of techniques to enhance the quality of the recordings.

音响师运用一系列技术来提高录音质量。

3. brawn [brɔːn] *n.* 体力

You need brains as well as brawn to do this job.

这项工作既需要脑力又需要体力。

4. holistic [hoʊ'lɪstɪk] *adj.* 全盘的,整体的;功能整体性的

So, as I said to you, natural medicine is also known as holistic medicine.

那么,正如我对你说过的那样,自然医学也被称为整体医学。

5. discipline ['dɪsəplɪn] *n.* 训练;训导;纪律;风纪;训练方法;行为准则;符合准则的行为;自制力

Online learning requires much time, commitment and discipline to keep up with the flow of the course.

线上学习要求学生花更多时间,专心致志,有自制力,这样才能与线上课程同步。

6. technique [tek'niːk] *n.* 技巧;技艺;工艺;技术;技能

She showed the technique to her students.

她向学生演示了那个技巧。

7. cudgel ['kʌdʒl] *n.* 棍棒;棍术;棒子;长棍

The yellow man carried his cudgel in his hand.

那个穿黄大衣的人,手里捏着他的棍子。

8. accumulate [əˈkjuːmjʊleɪt] *v.* 堆积,积累;(数量)逐渐增加,(质量)渐渐提高

I accumulated a roomful of documents and tape recordings.

我搜集了满屋子的文件和磁带录音。

9. philosophy [fəˈlɑːsəfi] *n.* 哲学;哲理;哲学体系,哲学思想;生活信条

He studied philosophy and psychology at Cambridge.

他在剑桥大学学习哲学和心理学。

10. immortal [ɪˈmɔːrtl] *n.* 不朽的人物;名垂千古的人物;神

Shakespeare is one of the immortals.

莎士比亚是不朽的人物之一。

三句必学 The more you practice, the more fluently you will speak.

1. People used **cudgels** to fight against wild beasts.

人们用棍棒来对抗野兽。

2. It is probably one of the earliest and longest lasting sports, which **utilizes** both brawn and brain.

这可能是最早和最持久的运动之一,它利用了体力和脑力。

3. The theory of Kungfu is based upon classical Chinese **philosophy**.

功夫理论是以中国古典哲学为基础的。

一篇必读 The more you read, the more knowledge you will get.

Chinese Kungfu, also known as wushu or Chinese **martial** arts, is an important part of traditional Chinese culture. It is probably one of the earliest and longest lasting sports, which **utilizes** both **brawn** and brain. Different from self-defense and boxing, Kungfu is more **holistic**, developing internal **discipline** with external **technique**.

People used **cudgels** to fight against wild beasts. Gradually they **accumulated** experience in self-defense. Over its long history, Chinese Kungfu has developed as a unique combination of exercise, practical self-defense, self-discipline and art. Chinese Kungfu is a large system of theory and practice, which combines techniques of self-defense and health-keeping.

The theory of Kungfu is based upon classical Chinese **philosophy**. Taijiquan is a Taoist internal martial art. One account of the history of taijiquan credits its development to the Taoist **immortal** Zhang Sanfeng, who is said to have drawn the inspiration for the art by watching a fight between a snake and an aggressive eagle.

1. Fill in the blanks.

People used _____ to fight against wild beasts. Gradually they _____ experience in self-defense. Over its long history it has _____ as a unique combination of exercise, practical self-defense, self-discipline, and art. Chinese Kungfu is a large _____ of theory and practice. It _____ techniques of self-defense and health-keeping.

2. Translate the following sentences.

（1）Chinese Kungfu is an important part of traditional Chinese culture.

_____

（2）Kungfu is more holistic, developing internal discipline with external technique.

_____

（3）Taijiquan is a Taoist internal martial art.

_____

3. Complete your group's speech draft.

Topic：Chinese Kungfu

轻松一刻 The more you share, the happier you will be.

Shaolin Kungfu is well known in China and abroad. The original purpose of Shaolin shadowboxing was keeping health, treating illness, protecting famous mountains, **safeguarding**（保护）ancient **temples**（寺庙）, self-defense, and **repelling**（击退）enemies. It boasts **diverse**（多样的）patterns, **plain**（朴素的）forms, and rich **internal**（内部的）and **external**（外部的）Kungfu.

Because of Kungfu TV series in the 1970s and movies about Shaolin Kungfu, this Buddhist temple in Henan Province became known around the world. The temple has a long history. It was destroyed, closed, reopened and rebuilt over and over.

Food in Chinese Culture

2-1 餐桌礼仪学一学 Chinese Dining Etiquette

中文导读

中国是一个传统的礼仪之邦,非常注重餐桌礼仪,比如吃饭的时候座次该怎么安排、该如何点菜、要如何吃菜才算有礼貌、如何敬酒、离席。

第一,入座的礼仪。先请客人入座上席,再请长者入座客人旁,其他人依次入座。

第二,进餐时的礼仪。先请客人、长者动筷子。夹菜时每次少一些,离自己远的菜就少吃一些,吃饭时不要发出声音,喝汤时也不要发出声响。

第三,进餐时不要打嗝,也不要出现其他声音。如果出现,就要说一声"真不好意思""对不起""请原谅"之类的话以示歉意。

第四,如果要给客人或长辈夹菜,最好用公筷,也可以把离客人或长辈远的菜肴送到他们跟前。

第五,吃到骨头等物时,不要往外面吐,也不要往地上扔,要慢慢用手拿到自己的碟子里。

第六,要适时地抽空和左右的人聊几句风趣的话以调和气氛。不要光顾着低头吃饭不管别人,也不要狼吞虎咽地大吃一顿,更不要贪杯。

第七,最好不要在餐桌上剔牙。如果要剔牙,就要用餐巾或手挡住自己的嘴巴。

第八,最后离席时,必须向主人表示感谢,或者就此时邀请主人以后到自己家做客以示回敬。

十个必背 The more you learn, the more you know.

1. **etiquette** [ˈetɪkət] *n.* 礼仪;(社会或行业中的)礼节;规矩

This goes against social etiquette.

这是违反社交常礼的。

2. **gobble** [ˈgɑːbl] *v.* 狼吞虎咽地吃

Pete gobbled all the beef stew.

皮特狼吞虎咽,把炖牛肉吃了个精光。

3. **dig** [dɪg] *v.* 挖掘,松土;整理;〈俚〉已理解

They tried digging in a patch just below the cave.

他们试着在洞穴正下方的一块地上挖掘。

4. **splash** [splæʃ] *v.* 泼洒;哗啦哗啦地溅

The kids were splashing through the puddles.

孩子们哗啦哗啦地溅着水花从水坑里蹚过。

5. swallow ['swɑːloʊ] *v.* 吞；咽下

He ate the apple so quickly that he almost swallowed the core.

他吃苹果太快，差点把核给吞了。

6. tissue ['tiʃu] *n.* 纸巾，面巾纸；(动、植物细胞的)组织

A tissue is a piece of thin soft paper that you use to blow your nose.

纸巾是指柔软的、薄的，用来擦鼻涕的纸。

7. tongue [tʌŋ] *n.* 舌头；舌

The dog's tongue was hanging out.

狗的舌头耷拉在外面。

8. sneeze [sniːz] *vi.* 打喷嚏

When we sneeze, our eyes close.

打喷嚏的时候眼睛会闭上。

9. refill [riːˈfɪl] *v.* 再注满；重新装满；再填；再补充

I refilled our wine glasses.

我再次斟满了我们的酒杯。

10. initiative [ɪˈnɪʃətɪv] *adj.* 自发的；创始的；初步的 *n.*(可数)倡议；新方案；主动性；积极性

Government initiatives to help young people have been inadequate.

政府在积极帮助年轻人方面做的还不够。

三句必学 The more you practice, the more fluently you will speak.

1. When finding the favorite dish, we can't **gobble** it up or put the plate in front of ourselves.

   当看到最喜欢的菜时，我们不能狼吞虎咽，也不能把菜放在自己面前。

2. Don't let the food **splash** or let soup or sauce drip onto the table.

   不要让食物飞溅，也不要让汤或酱汁滴到桌子上。

3. You should try to **refill** your bowl with rice yourself and take the initiative to fill the bowls of elders with rice and food from the dishes.

   你应该自己添饭，并且主动给长辈盛饭和夹菜。

一篇必读 The more you read, the more knowledge you will get.

As a guest at a meal, we should pay more attention to Chinese dining **etiquette**. At first, we should know the seating arrangement.

Let older people eat first, or if we hear an elder say "let's eat", we can start to eat. We should pick up the bowl with the left hand. When helping ourselves to the dishes, we should take food first from the plates in front of us. When finding the favorite dish, we can't **gobble** it up or put the plate in front of ourselves. It is bad manners to use the chopsticks to "**dig** for treasure" and eat like a horse.

Picking too much food at a time is not a good manner. Don't let the food **splash** or let soup or sauce drip onto the table. When eating, we should close the mouth to chew food well before **swallowing** it. If there is food around the mouth, use a **tissue** to wipe it, instead of licking it with the **tongue**. When chewing food, don't make noises. It is best not to talk with others with the mouth full.

If we want to cough or **sneeze**, please use the hand to cover the mouth and turn away. If we find something unpleasant in the mouth when chewing in the throat, we should leave the dinner table to spit it out. We should try to **refill** the bowl with rice ourselves and take the **initiative** to fill the bowls of elders with rice and food from the dishes.

1. Fill in the blanks.

It is not good _____ to pick up too much food at a time. Don't let the food _____ or let soup or sauce_____ onto the table. When eating, we should _____ the mouth to chew food well before _____ it. If there is food around the mouth, use a _____ to wipe it, instead _____ licking it with the _____. When chewing food, don't make _____. It is best not to talk with others with the mouth _____.

2. Tick out the polite behaviors.

(   ) When finding the favorite dish, we can put the plate in front of ourselves.

(   ) Don't talk with others with the mouth full.

(   ) If we want to cough or sneeze, use the hand to cover the mouth and turn away.

(   ) We should refill the bowl with rice by ourselves.

(   ) We should take the initiative to fill the bowls of elders with rice and food from the dishes.

3. Complete your group's speech draft.

Topic：Chinese Dining Etiquette

🎙 **轻松一刻 The more you share, the happier you will be.**

At Chinese **banquets**（宴会）, the seating arrangement is probably the most important part of Chinese dining **etiquette**（礼仪）, especially in Chinese business banquets. Generally, round tables are used at Chinese banquets and the seat facing the **entrance**（入口）is the seat of honor. The seats on the left hand side of the seat of honor are second, fourth, sixth, etc. in importance, while those on the right are third, fifth, seventh, etc. in importance. The seat of honor, **reserved**（保留）for the master of the banquet or the guests with highest status, is the one in the **center**（中心）facing east or facing the entrance. Those of higher position sit closer to the seat of honor. The guests of the lowest position sit furthest from the seat of honor.

2-2 中国名菜品一品 Popular Chinese Dishes

中文导读

　　中国菜是中国各地区、各民族各种菜肴的总称，具有历史悠久、技术精湛、品类丰富、流派众多、风格独特的特点，是中国烹饪数千年发展的结晶，在世界上享有盛誉。中国菜是中国烹饪、中国饮食文化的重要组成部分之一，又称中华食文化、世界三大菜系（中国菜、法国菜、土耳其菜）之一，深远地影响了东亚地区的饮食及其文化。

十个必背 The more you learn, the more you know.

1. specialty [ˈspɛʃəlti] *n.* 专业，专长；特点，特别事项；特性，特质；[律]盖印的契约

What's your specialty today?

你们今天有什么特色食品？

2. ingredient [ɪnˈɡriːdɪənt] *n.* 成分；（尤指烹饪）原料；（成功的）因素，要素

Mix all the ingredients well.

把所有原料搅拌均匀。

3. dice [daɪs] *v.* 切成丁；将（肉、菜等）切成小方块

She diced the carrots for the soup.

她把胡萝卜切成细丁做汤。

4. garlic [ˈɡɑːrlɪk] *n.* 蒜；大蒜

You can taste the garlic in this stew.

在这炖肉里你可以尝出大蒜的味道。

5. spicy [ˈspaɪsi] *adj.* 辛辣的；加有香料的

Spicy food is not good for my stomach.

辛辣的食物对我的胃不好。

6. pepper [ˈpɛpɚ] *n.* 辣椒；胡椒；胡椒粉

Season with salt and pepper.

用盐和胡椒调味。

7. condiment [ˈkɑːndɪmənt] *n.* 调味品，佐料

The condiment industry mainly includes the following fields: chicken essence, soy sauce and complex condiment.

调味料行业主要有以下几个领域：鸡精、酱油和复合调味料。

8. crispy [ˈkrɪspi] *adj.* 脆的；酥脆的；鲜脆的

How do we make crispy pork chop?

如何炸出酥脆美味的猪排？

9. pancake [ˈpænˌkeik] *n.* 烙饼，薄煎饼；粉饼；[航]平降，平坠

The pancake is burnt.

饼烤焦了。

10. savory [ˈseɪvərɪ] *adj.* 咸的；好吃的

I've ordered savory pork and cole slaw.

我点了咸猪肉和凉拌生菜丝。

三句必学 The more you practice, the more fluently you will speak.

1. Kung Pao Chicken（宫保鸡丁）is a famous Sichuan-style specialty, popular with both Chinese and foreigners.

   宫保鸡丁是著名的川菜特色菜，深受中外游客的喜爱。

2. Ma Po Tofu（麻婆豆腐）is one of the most famous dishes in Chuan Cuisine with a history of more than 100 years.

   麻婆豆腐是川菜中最著名的菜肴之一，已有100多年的历史。

3. Peking Roasted Duck（北京烤鸭）is savored for its thin and **crispy** skin.

   北京烤鸭因其薄而脆的皮而受到人们的喜爱。

一篇必读 The more you read, the more knowledge you will get.

The following are popular dishes among Chinese and people from other culture backgrounds.

Kung Pao Chicken（宫保鸡丁）is a famous Sichuan-style **specialty**, popular with both Chinese and foreigners. The major **ingredients** are **diced** chicken, dried chili and fried peanuts. People in Western countries have created a Western-style Kung Pao Chicken, for which they coat the diced chicken with cornstarch and add vegetables, sweet and sour sauce and mashed **garlic**.

Ma Po Tofu（麻婆豆腐）is one of the most famous dishes in Chuan Cuisine with a history of more than 100 years. Ma（麻）describes a **spicy** and hot taste which comes from **pepper** powder, one kind of **condiment** usually used in Chuan Cuisine. The milky tofu is enriched with brownish red ground beef and chopped green onion. It is really a tasty delicacy.

Peking Roasted Duck（北京烤鸭）is a famous dish from Beijing and it is considered as one of China's national dishes. Peking duck is savored for its thin and **crispy** skin. The sliced Peking Duck is often eaten with **pancakes**, sweet bean sauce or soy with mashed garlic. It is a must-taste dish in Beijing!

Spring Rolls（春卷）are made of round spring roll wrappers and rolled into a cylindrical shape. The fillings could be vegetables or meat, and the taste could be either sweet or **savory**. After fillings are wrapped, the next step is to fry. Deep-fried spring rolls can be golden in color. It is a dish especially popular in Jiangxi, Jiangsu, Shanghai, Fujian, Guangzhou, Shenzhen, Hong Kong, etc.

1. Describe each dish in one sentence.

Kung Pao Chicken（宫保鸡丁）_____

Ma Po Tofu（麻婆豆腐）_____

Peking Roasted Duck（北京烤鸭）_____

Spring Rolls（春卷）_____

2. Write advertising slogans for each dish.

Dish	Food ingredients	An Advertising Slogan For the Dish

3. Complete your group's speech draft.

Topic: The Most Popular Chinese Dish

🔊 **轻松一刻 The more you share, the happier you will be.**

China is rich in tourist attractions. Delicious foods are important in a good tour. With a long history, Chinese **cuisine**（菜肴）is one important part of Chinese culture. A meal in Chinese culture **consists**（由……组成）of two parts: a **carbohydrate**（碳水化合物）**source**（来源）and dishes of vegetables, meat, fish, or other items. Chinese dishes are famous for color, aroma, taste, meaning and appearance.

Chinese cuisine originated from different regions of China. Regional cultural differences **vary**（变化）greatly among the different regions of China, giving rise to the different styles of food. There are eight main regional cuisines.

They are Anhui, Fujian, Guangdong, Hunan, Jiangsu, Shangdong, Sichuan and Zhejiang. The regional cooking styles are as diverse as the terrain and its people. Naturally, they are also strongly influenced by the **staple**（主要的）crops that grow in each specific region.

Chinese cuisine has become **widespread**（分布广的）in many other parts of the world—from East Asia to North America, Australasia and Western Europe.

2-3 特色小吃尝一尝 Popular Chinese Snacks

中文导读

　　小吃是一类在口味上具有特定风格特色的食品的总称。小吃就地取材,能够突出反映当地的文化及社会生活风貌,也是离乡游子们寄托家乡思念的主要对象。

　　世界各地都有各种各样的风味小吃,因当地风俗而异,特色鲜明,风味独特。现代人吃小吃通常不是为了吃饱。除了可以解馋,还可以借品尝异地风味小吃了解当地风土人情。

　　中华名小吃,是指中餐里面具有地域性和民俗性的,通过蒸、炸、煮、烙、煎、烤、烧、炒等烹饪技法制作的,不属于大菜类和一般主食面点的风味饮食制品,并经过美食专家评论组按照相应评选程序评选而出。

十个必背 The more you learn, the more you know.

1. snack [snæk] *n.* 点心;小吃;快餐;易办到的事

A snack is something such as a chocolate bar that you eat between meals.

零食是你在两餐之间吃的东西,比如巧克力。

2. bun [bʌn] *n.* 圆形的小面包或点心

You cannot eat a bun in one bite.

你不能一口吃下一个面包。

3. steam [stiːm] *v.* 蒸(食物)

A fly was hovering above a steamed bun.

一只苍蝇在馒头上面飞来飞去。

4. entire [ɪnˈtaɪər] *adj.* 全部的;整个的;完全的

Latest reports say that mud slides buried entire villages.

最新报道说泥石流掩埋了整个村庄。

5. spin [spɪn] *v.* (使)快速旋转

Next to us, a couple twirled and spun in elegant circles.

在我们旁边,一对夫妇一圈又一圈快速优美地旋转着。

6. sticky [ˈstɪki] *adj.* 黏(性)的

Stir in the milk to make a soft but not sticky dough.

把牛奶搅进去,和成软而不黏的面团。

7. melt [melt] *v.* 熔化;(使)融化

The snow was beginning to melt.

积雪开始融化了。

8. expose [ɪkˈspoʊz] *vt.* 暴露;揭露;露出

The enemy were exposed to our machine gun fire.

敌人暴露在我军的机枪火力之下。

9. liquid [ˈlɪkwɪd] *n.* 液体

It's vital not to overheat the liquid.

最关键的是不要让液体过热。

10. glutinous [ˈɡluːtənəs] *adj.* 黏的;胶质的

The sauce was glutinous and tasted artificial.

这种酱有些黏,尝起来不是很地道。

三句必学 The more you practice, the more fluently you will speak.

1. Dragon's Beard Candy（龙须酥）is not only a type of Chinese candy, but it is also considered as a traditional art originating in the Han Dynasty.

   龙须酥不仅是中国糖果的一种,而且被认为是起源于汉代的一种传统艺术。

2. A skewer with crabapples is dipped in liquid sugar and then it is dried.

   将野果用竹签串成串后蘸上麦芽糖稀,糖稀遇风迅速变硬。

3. It is made from **glutinous** rice flour mixed with a small amount of water to form balls.

   它由糯米粉和少量水混合而成,呈球状。

一篇必读 The more you read, the more knowledge you will get.

Desserts in China are quite different from in the West.

Red Bean Bun（豆沙包）

Red bean buns are a popular sweet version of the **steamed** buns, filled with red bean paste. The buns come in a variety of different shapes and sizes. They are popular throughout the **entire** country, but especially popular in the north of China. We can get them in a restaurant, steamed in different shapes, or we can get them in the supermarket for on the go.

Dragon's Beard Candy（龙须酥）

Dragon's Beard Candy is not only a type of Chinese candy, but it is also considered as a traditional art originating in the Han Dynasty. It is made of **spun** sugar and it is very **sticky**. It **melts** easily. When it is **exposed** to high temperatures, it becomes even stickier. This food is generally sold by the side of the road or at stalls near popular tourist destinations.

Tanghulu（糖葫芦）—**Candied Fruit on a Stick**

Tanghulu, the "Chinese toffee apple" is an old Beijing-style snack. A skewer（肉串扦子）with crabapples is dipped in **liquid** sugar and then it is dried. Common varieties include other fruits coated（给……涂上一层）in sugar, such as kiwi fruit or grapes. We can buy from carts by the side of the street. We can find it easily at common tourist sites in Beijing.

Tangyuan（汤圆）—Sweet Soup Balls

Tangyuan is a Chinese dessert. It is made from **glutinous** rice flour mixed with a small amount of water to form balls. We can fill a glutinous rice ball with either sweet or savory fillings. It is cooked and served in boiling water. Its history can trace back to the Song Dynasty. Tangyuan is a traditional food eaten during the Lantern Festival.

1. Describe each dessert in one sentence.

Red Bean Bun _____

Dragon's Beard Candy _____.

Tanghulu_____

Tangyuan_____

2. Draw each dessert promotion poster with key words.

Red Bean Bun	Dragon's Beard Candy
Tanghulu	Tangyuan

3. Complete your group's speech draft.

Topic：The Most Popular Chinese Dessert

轻松一刻 The more you share, the happier you will be.

Huamo, also known as "mianhua", is a Chinese folk **flour sculpture**（面塑品）. Wenxi huamo is the traditional name of Wenxi County, Yuncheng City, Shanxi Province. It is named for its various styles. Wenxi huamo was popular in the Ming and Qing Dynasties. It has a history of more than 1,000 years and has formed a unique **artistic**（艺术）style and a complete creative system.

Huamo is also famous for its **delicacy**（美味）. Wenxi huamo has four series of "huagao", "huamo", "mascot" and "dish top", with more than 200 varieties. It was listed as a **national intangible cultural heritage**（国家级非物质文化遗产）in 2008 and **exhibited**（展出）at the Shanghai World Expo in 2010. Four world records were set at the China Wenxi Huamo Cultural Festival held in 2012.

2-4　拿起筷子试一试 Chinese Chopsticks

中文导读

　　三千年前,筷子已经出现在我们祖先的餐桌上,用以辅助进食,"筯""箸""梜"这些词便是"筷子"说法的原型。

　　首先,筷子必须一头圆、一头方。圆象征天,方象征地,对应"天圆地方",这是中国人对世界基本原则的理解。中国人讲究"阴阳两和""合二为一",意求圆满,这种暗含"灵与肉""理想与现实"相结合的观念,在筷子上得以显现,才有了"一双筷子"的说法。中国筷子形状近似长方体或圆柱体,较长且厚重,标准长度是七寸六分,象征人的"七情六欲",材质多为木质或竹质,也有用象牙、红木、金银等名贵材料制作的工艺品箸,更善运用各雕刻工艺,彰显典雅,极具古典气质。

　　中国人在用筷方面也有诸多讲究,如:一双筷不能长短不一,否则就是"三长两短",这是大不吉利的;盛饭之碗应当用手捧之,忌用筷敲击碗沿;用筷插或不断翻拨菜品,是十分失礼不雅之举;等等。用筷礼仪是中国筷子文化的一面。

十个必背 The more you learn, the more you know.

1. chopstick [ˈtʃɑːpstɪk] *n.* 筷子

The Chinese eat with chopsticks.

中国人用筷子吃饭。

2. resemble [rɪˈzɛmbəl] *v.* 与……相像,类似于

Some of the commercially produced venison resembles beef in flavor.

有些商业化养殖的鹿肉味道和牛肉很相似。

3. pronunciation [prəˌnʌnsiˈeʃən] *n.* 发音;读法;发音方法;发音方式

She gave the word its French pronunciation.

她读出了该词的法语发音。

4. newlyweds [ˈnuliˌwɛdz] *n.* 新婚夫妇

He led the way in drinking the health of the newlyweds.

他带头为新郎新娘的健康祝酒。

5. taper [ˈteɪpər] *v.* (使)逐渐变窄

The tail tapered to a rounded tip.

尾部越来越细,最后成了个圆尖。

6. protrude [prəʊ'truːd] *v.* 使突出;使伸出

The tip of her tongue was protruding slightly.

她的舌尖微微伸出。

7. thumb [θʌm] *n.* 拇指;(手套的)拇指部分

She bit the tip of her left thumb, not looking at me.

她咬着左手的拇指尖,眼睛也不看我。

8. separate ['sepəreɪt] *v.* 分开;(使)分离;区分;隔开

Each villa has a separate sitting-room.

每栋别墅都有一间独立的起居室。

9. exert [ɪg'zɜːrt] *v.* 发挥;运用;使受(影响等);用(力)

He exerted considerable influence on the thinking of the scientific community on these issues.

他极大地影响了科学界对这些问题的看法。

10. pressure ['preʃər] *n.* 压力;挤压;压强;大气压

The pressure of work is beginning to get to him.

工作的压力使他烦恼。

三句必学 The more you practice, the more fluently you will speak.

1. Having babies quickly is a popular good wish in China for **newly married couples**.

在中国,早生贵子是对新婚夫妇的美好祝福。

2. Pick up food by moving the upper **chopstick** and holding the lower chopstick still.

通过移动筷子的上半部分并保持下半部分不动来拾取食物。

3. To separate a piece of food into two pieces, **exert** controlled pressure on the chopsticks while moving them apart from each other.

为了把食物一分为二,需要筷子上均匀用力,把食物分开。

一篇必读 The more you read, the more knowledge you will get.

Chopsticks are called kuaizi(筷子) in Chinese, which **resembles** the **pronunciation** of two other words "soon" (快 kuài) and "son(s)" (子 zǐ). Having babies quickly is a popular good wish in China for newly married couples. Therefore, it is a tradition in some areas to give chopsticks as a gift to **newlyweds**. Chopsticks are usually made with a round end and a square end, or with one end **tapered**.

There is not just one right way to use chopsticks. Do you know how to hold and use chopsticks?

①Put the unmoving chopstick with the food end **protruding** 5-15 cm on the 4th finger with the middle of your **thumb** on top to hold it still.

②Hold the movable chopstick in the same way you would hold a pen to write, but with the end protruding more from the finger tips.

③Pick up food by moving the upper chopstick and holding the lower chopstick still.

④To **separate** a piece of food into two pieces, **exert** controlled **pressure** on the chopsticks while moving them apart from each other. This needs a lot of practice.

1. Fill in the blanks.

_____ are called kuaizi（筷子）in Chinese, which **resemble**s the _____ of two other words: "soon"（快 kuài）and "son(s)"（子 zǐ）. It is a popular good _____ in China for newly _____ _____ couples to have babies quickly. Therefore, it is a _____ in some areas to give chopsticks as a gift to _____. Chopsticks are usually made with a round _____ and a square end, or with one end _____.

2. Tick out the right way to use chopsticks.

(　　) Put the movable chopstick with the food end protruding 5-15 cm on the 4th finger with the middle of your thumb on top to hold it still.

(　　) Hold the unmoving chopstick in the same way you would hold a pen to write, but with the end protruding more from the finger tips.

(　　) Pick up food by moving the upper chopstick and holding the lower chopstick still.

(　　) To separate a piece of food into two pieces, exert controlled pressure on the chopsticks while moving them apart from each other.

3. Complete your group's speech draft.

Topic：How to Use Chopsticks

轻松一刻 The more you share, the happier you will be.

Taboos（禁忌）—Five Tips for Using Chopsticks

When using chopsticks to eat, people need to pay attention to some taboos and common conventions:

1. Don't point your chopsticks at others. This is seen as a sign of **disrespect**（不尊重）. Likewise, don't wave your chopsticks around in the air or play with them while eating.

2. Don't knock on **tableware**（餐具）with chopsticks: this is seen as a sign of begging.

3. Don't **stir**（搅拌）food with your chopsticks to find what you want. This is very rude.

4. Don't **invert**（倒转）your chopsticks, i.e. use them the wrong way round.

5. Never stick chopsticks into your food, especially not into rice. Only at **funerals**（葬礼）are chopsticks stuck into rice on an **altar**（祭坛）, where they look like joss sticks, also burnt on the altar for the dead.

2-5 宫保鸡丁做一做 Kung Pao Chicken

中文导读

　　宫保鸡丁,是一道闻名中外的特色传统名菜,鲁菜、川菜、黔菜中都有收录。各菜系中的宫保鸡丁原料、做法都有差别。宫保鸡丁的起源与鲁菜中的酱爆鸡丁、黔菜的胡辣子鸡丁有关,后该菜式经清代山东巡抚、四川总督丁宝桢改良发扬,形成了一道新菜式——宫保鸡丁,并流传至今。此道菜也被归类为北京宫廷菜。之后宫保鸡丁也流传到国外。

　　宫保鸡丁选用鸡肉为主料,佐以花生米、黄瓜、辣椒等辅料烹制而成,红而不辣、辣而不猛、香辣味浓、肉质滑脆。

　　2018年9月,宫保鸡丁被评为"中国菜"之贵州十大经典名菜、四川十大经典名菜之一。

十个必背 The more you learn, the more you know.

1. ingredient [ɪŋˈriːdɪrnts] *n.* 组成部分;(烹调的)原料;(构成)要素;因素

I'd already measured out the ingredients.

我已经量好了配料。

2. seasoning [ˈsiːznɪŋz] *n.* 调味品,佐料

Beef, mushrooms and onions stewed in red wine and seasonings.

牛肉、蘑菇和洋葱在红葡萄酒和香料中炖制。

3. chili [chili] *n.* 红辣椒

Of course. I like chilies and Sichuan food.

当然了。我喜欢吃辣椒和川菜。

4. ginger [ˈdʒɪndʒɚ] *n.* 姜黄色;姜,生姜;精力,活力

I live mostly on coffee and ginger ale.

我主要喝咖啡和姜汁汽水。

5. garlic [ˈɡɑːrlɪk] *n.* 大蒜;蒜头

Boil the chick peas, add garlic and lemon juice.

把鹰嘴豆放在开水中煮,并加入大蒜和柠檬汁。

6. vinegar [ˈvɪnɪɡə] 醋;乖戾,尖酸刻薄;〈口〉充沛的精力

If the sauce seems too sweet, add a dash of red wine vinegar.

如果酱汁太甜的话,可以加少许红酒醋。

7. **starch** [stɑːrtʃ] *n.* 淀粉,含淀粉的食物;形式主义;古板,僵硬;元气

   She reorganized her eating so that she was taking more fruit and vegetables and less starch, salt, and fat.

   她重新调整了她的饮食,多吃水果和蔬菜,少吃淀粉、盐和脂肪。

8. **chop** [tʃɑːp] *v.* 切碎,砍;向下猛击;降低;终止

   Chop the butter into small pieces.

   把黄油切成小片。

9. **drain** [dreɪn] *v.* 排水;排空;(使)流光;放干;(使)流走,流出

   The water slowly drained away, down through the porous soil.

   水慢慢流走了,渗入了疏松的土壤。

10. **stir-fry** [ˈstɜːr fraɪ] *vt.* 翻炒;炒;煸

    Stir-fry the vegetables until crisp.

    将蔬菜煸炒至变脆。

三句必学 The more you practice, the more fluently you will speak.

1. Mix the chicken cubes with the cooking wine, cooking **starch** and salt for half an hour.

   将裹满料酒的鸡块、烹饪淀粉和盐混合腌制半小时。

2. Use oil to fry the peanuts and **drain** them. Set them on a plate to cool.

   用油炸花生,然后沥干。把它们放在盘子里冷却。

3. Add the starchy sauce and chopped green onions. Re-add the cool fried peanuts. **Stir-fry** together for 30 seconds.

   加入芡汁和葱花,再加入凉下来的花生米。煸炒30秒就可以装盘了。

一篇必读 The more you read, the more knowledge you will get.

Kung Pao Chicken is a famous Chinese dish made with diced chicken, chilies, and peanuts.

❖ **Ingredients and Seasonings**

Main ingredients: 400−500 g chicken, 100 g peanuts

Seasonings: dried red **chilies**, 5 green onions, a piece of **ginger**, 5 pieces of **garlic**, 30 g cooking oil, 15 g thick broad-bean sauce, 5 g cooking wine, 15 g cooking starch, 2 g salt, 5 g rice **vinegar**, 10 g soy sauce and 5 g sugar

The amounts of the seasonings can be adjusted according to personal taste.

(Omit the chilies for a non-spicy Kung Pao Chicken.)

❖ **Preparation**

①Clean the chicken breasts and dice them.

②Mix the chicken cubes with the cooking wine, cooking **starch** and salt for half an hour.

③Soak peanuts in hot water for 10 minutes and remove the peanut skins.

④Cut chilies into small pieces. **Chop** the green onions. Dice the ginger and garlic.

⑤Make a bowl of starchy sauce with the sugar, soy sauce, rice vinegar, and cooking wine.

❖ **Cooking Instructions**

①Use oil to fry the peanuts and drain them. Set them on a plate to cool.

②Heat oil in a hot wok（炒菜锅）over high heat. Fry the chicken cubes until they turn slightly brown. **Drain** them and remove them to a plate.

③**Stir-fry** the dried chilies for 30 seconds to release the spice.

④Re-add the fried chicken cubes and add the diced garlic, ginger and the thick broad-bean sauce. Stir-fry until the sauce becomes red.

⑤Add the starchy sauce and chopped green onions. Re-add the cool fried peanuts. Stir-fry together for 30 seconds.

⑥Serve it on a plate.

1. Translate ingredients and seasonings.

chicken_____ peanut_____ dried red chilies_____ green onions_____

ginger_____garlic_____ cooking oil_____ thick broad-bean sauce_____

cooking wine_____ cooking starch_____ salt_____ rice vinegar_____ soy sauce_____ sugar_____

2. Draw a mind-map of cooking Kung Pao Chicken.

3. Complete your group's speech draft.

Topic：How to Cook Kung Pao Chicken

🐌 轻松一刻 **The more you share, the happier you will be.**

The Origin of Kung Pao Chicken

It is said that the dish was created by Ding Baozhen（1820-1886）, a **governor**（管辖者）of Sichuan Province during the Qing Dynasty. He liked eating chicken and peanuts, and especially loved spicy flavors. He created a **delicacy**（佳肴）made of diced chicken, red chilies, and peanuts.

Ding Baozhen was a good governor during his 10-year service in Sichuan, **contributing**（做贡献）a lot to the local people's **wellbeing**（幸福）. So the Qing government gave him an official title: Kung Pao. Therefore, Ding's delicacy was named "Kung Pao Chicken" to **commemorate**（纪念）his great contributions.

Chapter 3

Festivals in Chinese Culture

3-1　中国节日道一道 Public Holidays in China

中文导读

节日是人类社会生活的枢纽,是人类物质文明与精神文明的载体。历经千百年岁月沧桑的传统节日,更是一个民族成熟文明的缩影,它既体现着人与自然的关系,又反映着现实的人与人的联系。就中国节日而言,它既是中国人长期不懈地探索自然规律的产物,包含着大量科学的天文、气象和物候知识,也是中华文明的哲学思想、审美意识和道德伦理在民俗风情上的集中体现。我们的先人综合太阳和月亮与人和自然的关系来确定节日的时间,可以说是人与自然的关系最好的体现。

千百年来,节日民俗给中国人一种井然有序的时间节奏、热闹而不失尺度的空间分布。节日得以存在和发展离不开一个民族主体的精神活动。虽然中国是一个人口众多的国度,中国人也以一种勤勉、节俭的方式过着自己的日子,但庸常的世俗生活因为有了热闹的节日,才构成中国人完整的生活,使每个人的人生因充满着期待、愉悦而显得非同寻常。

十个必背 The more you learn, the more you know.

1. **complicated** ['kɑ:mplɪkeɪtɪd] *adj.* 结构复杂的;混乱的,麻烦的

   The situation in Lebanon is very complicated.

   黎巴嫩的情况十分复杂。

2. **encourage** [ɪn'kɜ:rɪdʒ] *v.* 促进;支持;鼓励,鼓舞;鼓动

   When things aren't going well, he encourages me, telling me not to give up.

   事情进展不顺的时候,他鼓励我说不要放弃。

3. **peak** [pik] *v.* 达到高峰,达到最大值;消瘦;变憔悴 *adj.* 峰(值)的;高峰的

   Temperatures have peaked at thirty degrees Celsius.

   温度最高达30摄氏度。

4. **tourism** ['tʊrɪzəm] *n.* 旅游业;观光业

   Tourism is a major source of income for the area.

   旅游业是这个地区的主要收入来源。

5. **scheme** [ski:m] *n.* 计划;方案

   The service is being expanded following the success of a pilot scheme.

   在试验性方案获得成功后,这项服务正在推广中。

6. calendar [ˈkæləndɚ] *n.* 日历;历法;日程表

There was a calendar on the wall above, with large squares around the dates.

上面的墙上挂着日历,日期上画着大大的方框。

7. applicable [ˈæplɪkəbəl,əˈplɪkəbl] *adj.* 适当的;可应用的

What is a reasonable standard for one family is not applicable for another.

对一个家庭合理的标准并不适用于另一个家庭。

8. labor [ˈleɪbɚ] *n.* 劳动;(尤指)体力劳动;任务;(一段时间的)工作;(统称)劳工,工人;劳动力

Every man should receive a fair price for the product of his labor.

每个人的劳动成果都应该获得合理的回报。

9. congress [ˈkɑːŋɡrəs] *n.* 代表大会

The National People's Congress is elected for a term of five years.

全国人民代表大会每届任期5年。

10. military [ˈmɪləteri] *adj.* 军事的;军队的;武装的 *n.* 军人;军队;军方

My husband was a military man all his life.

我丈夫一生都是军人。

三句必学 The more you practice, the more fluently you will speak.

1. The week-long holidays on May (Labor) Day and National Day began in 2000, as a measure to increase and **encourage** holiday expenditure.

   劳动节和国庆节放假一周的规定始于2000年,作为增加和鼓励假日消费的措施。

2. The resulting seven-day holidays are called "**Golden Weeks**"(黄金周), and have become **peak** seasons for travel and **tourism**.

   由此产生的七天假期被称为"黄金周",并成为旅游旺季。

3. In 2008, the Labor Day holiday was shortened to three days to reduce travel rushes to just twice a year, and instead, three traditional Chinese holidays were added.

   2008年,劳动节假期被缩短到三天,来将每年的旅游高峰降至仅两次,反而增加了三个中国传统节日。

一篇必读 The more you read, the more knowledge you will get.

Holidays in China are **complicated**. The week-long holidays on May (Labor) Day and National Day began in 2000, as a measure to increase and **encourage** holiday expenditure. The resulting seven-day holidays are called "**Golden Weeks**"(黄金周), and have become **peak** seasons for travel and **tourism**. In 2008, the Labor Day holiday was shortened to three days to reduce travel rushes to just twice a year, and instead, three traditional Chinese holidays were added.

The following is a traditional holiday **scheme**.

Date	English name	Local name	Remarks
January 1	New Year's Day	元旦	
1st day of 1st Lunar month	Spring Festival (Chinese New Year)	春节	Based on Chinese calendar. Holidays last two full weeks, up to the Lantern Festival.
15th day of 1st Lunar month	Lantern Festival	元宵节	Based on Chinese calendar.
March 8	International Women's Day	国际妇女节	**Applicable** to Women（half-day）.
March 12	Arbor Day	植树节	Also known as National Tree Planting Day.
5th Solar Term（usually April 4-6）	Tomb Sweeping Day	清明节	Based on the Qingming solar term.
May 1	Labor Day	劳动节	International Workers Day.
May 4	Youth Day	青年节	Applicable to youth from the age of 14 to 28（half-day）. Commemorating the May 4th Movement.
June 1	Children's Day	"六一"儿童节	Applicable to children below the age of 14（1 day）.
5th day of 5th Lunar month	Dragon Boat Festival	端午节	Based on Chinese calendar.
July 1	the Communist Party of China（CPC）Founding Day	建党节	Formation of 1st National Congress in July 1921.
August 1	People's Liberation Army（PLA）Day	建军节	Nanchang Uprising（南昌起义）on August 1, 1927. **Military** personnel in active service（half-day）.
7th day of 7th Lunar month	Double Seven Festival	七夕节	The Chinese Valentine's Day, based on Chinese **calendar**.
15th day of 7th Lunar month	Spirit Festival (Ghost Festival)	中元节	Based on Chinese calendar.
15th day of 8th Lunar month	Mid-Autumn Festival	中秋节	Based on Chinese calendar.
October 1	National Day	国庆节	Founding of PRC on October 1, 1949.
9th day of 9th Lunar month	Double Ninth Festival	重阳节	Based on Chinese calendar.

1. Match the name and time of Chinese festival.

A. October 1	1. Spring Festival	a. 国庆节
B. May 1	2. Lantern Festival	b. 元宵节
C. 5th Solar Term	3. Tomb Sweeping Day	c. 七夕节
D. 15th day of 1st Lunar month	4. Labor Day	d. 重阳节
E. 5th day of 5th Lunar month	5. Dragon Boat Festival	e. 端午节
F. 1st day of 1st Lunar month	6. Double Seven Festival	f. 春节

G. 15th day of 8th Lunar month	7. Mid-Autumn Festival	g. 中秋节
H. 7th day of 7th Lunar month	8. National Day	h. 劳动节
I. 9th day of 9th Lunar month	9. Double Ninth Festival	i. 清明节

2. Fill in the blanks.

The week-long holidays on Labor Day and National Day began in 2000, as a _____ to increase and _____ holiday spending. The resulting seven-day holidays are called "_____", and have become _____ seasons for travel and tourism. In 2008, the Labor Day holiday was _____ to three days to _____ travel rushes to just twice a year, and instead, three _____ Chinese holidays were _____.

3. Complete your group's speech draft.

Topic：Public Holidays in China

🌐 轻松一刻 **The more you share, the happier you will be.**

Ethnic Minorities Holidays

There are public holidays celebrated by certain ethnic minorities in certain regions, which are decided by local governments. The following are holidays at province-level divisions.

Date	English name	Chinese name	Ethnic Groups	Remarks
1st day of Tibetan year	Losar	洛萨/藏历新年	**Tibetan**（藏族）	7 days in Tibet
June 6th of Tibetan calendar	Sho Dun	雪顿节	Tibetan	1 day in Tibet
October 1st of Islamic calendar	Eid ul-Fitr	开斋节/肉孜节	Hui, **Uyghur**（维吾尔族）and other **Muslims**（穆斯林）	2 days for all in Ningxia; 1 day for Muslims（only）in Xinjiang
December 10th of Islamic calendar	Eid al-Adha	古尔邦节	Hui, Uyghur and other Muslims	2 days for all in Ningxia; 3 days for Muslims, 1 day for others in Xinjiang
the 3rd day of the 3rd Lunisolar month	Sam Nyied Sam	三月三	Zhuang	3 days in Guangxi

3-2　新春佳节聚一聚 Chinese New Year

中文导读

　　春节是指中国传统的农历新年,俗称"年节",传统名称为新年、大年、新岁,口头上又称度岁、庆新岁、过年。中国人过春节已有4000多年的历史。在现代,人们把春节定于农历正月初一,但一般至少要到正月十五(上元节),新年才算结束。在民间,传统意义上的春节是指从腊月的腊祭、腊月二十三或二十四的祭灶,一直到正月十九。

　　春节期间,中国的汉族和一些少数民族都要举行各种庆祝活动。这些活动均以祭祀神佛、祭奠祖先、除旧布新、迎禧接福、祈求丰年为主要内容,形式丰富多彩,带有浓郁的民族特色。受到中华文化的影响,属于汉字文化圈的一些其他国家和民族也有庆祝春节的习俗。人们在春节这一天都尽可能地回到家里和亲人团聚,表达对未来一年的热切期盼和对新一年生活的美好祝福。

　　春节是中华民族最隆重的传统佳节,同时也是中国人情感得以释放、心理诉求得以满足的重要载体,是中华民族一年一度的狂欢节和永远的精神支柱。春节与清明节、端午节、中秋节并称为中国四大传统节日。

十个必背 The more you learn, the more you know.

1. weaken [ˈwiːkən] *v.* (使)虚弱,衰弱;减弱;削弱;(使)减弱;动摇;犹豫

Nothing could weaken his resolve to continue.

什么也不能削弱他继续下去的决心。

2. worship [ˈwɜːrʃɪp] *v.* 崇拜,尊崇;爱慕

She had worshiped him for years.

她仰慕他已有多年。

3. blessing [ˈblesɪŋ] *n.* 上帝的恩宠;祝福;祝颂;赞同

I send my blessings every day and remember that I love you very much.

我每天都祝福着你们,记住,我非常爱你们。

4. decoration [ˌdekəˈreɪʃn] *n.* 装饰

With its simple decoration, the main bedroom is a peaceful haven.

主卧室装饰简单,像一处宁静的港湾。

5. couplet [ˈkʌplɪt] *n.* 对联;对句

This antithetical couplet is my father's handwriting.

这幅对联是父亲的亲笔。

6. ancestor [ˈænˌsɛstə] *n.* 祖先,祖宗;被继承人;原型;(动物的)原种,先祖

He could trace his ancestors back seven hundred years.

他的先祖可以上溯到700年前。

7. gala [ˈgɑːlə] *n.* 庆祝;节日

Our school held a New Year's Gala.

我们的学校举行了新年联欢晚会。

8. firecracker [ˈfaɪərkrækər] *n.* 鞭炮;爆竹

He heard the sound of distant firecrackers.

他听到了远处的爆竹声。

9. envelope [ˈenvəloʊp] *n.* 信封;塑料封套;塑料封皮

I put "please forward" on the envelope.

我在信封上写了"请转递"。

10. retiree [rɪˌtaɪəˈriː] *n.* 退休人员

Some retirees enjoy their daily routine; they feel as free as birds.

一些退休者,自由自在,享受悠闲的日常生活。

三句必学 The more you practice, the more fluently you will speak.

1. Chinese people clean their houses, which welcomes good fortune in new year.
中国人打扫房子迎接新一年中的好运。

2. After reunion dinner, families normally sit together to watch the Spring Festival **Gala.**
团圆饭之后,一家人通常坐在一起看春节联欢晚会。

3. It has long been a Chinese tradition to set off **firecrackers** from the first minute of their new year.
新年一到就开始放鞭炮,这是中国人的传统。

一篇必读 The more you read, the more knowledge you will get.

Spring Festival is China's most important festival. Chinese New Year is a time for families to be together. Wherever they are, people are expected to be home to celebrate the festival with their families. It's celebrated for 16 days, from the Eve to Lantern Festival. Many customs are still followed today, but others have **weakened.**

Preparing for Chinese New Year

Chinese **worship** the Kitchen God on the 23rd of the 12th lunar month to pray for **blessings** on their home life. Chinese people clean their houses, which welcomes good fortune in new year. Home **decoration** is done on Chinese New Year's Eve. Red **couplet**s are pasted on doors.

Having the Reunion Dinner

The New Year's Eve dinner is the most important meal of the year. Dishes with lucky meanings must be included in the dinner such as fish, dumplings, and spring rolls. Some Chinese worship their **ancestors** before the dinner, to show that they are putting their ancestors first.

Staying Up for Midnight

Chinese have the custom of staying up late on New Year's Eve to welcome our new year's arrival. After reunion dinner, families normally sit together to watch the Spring Festival **Gala.** At the same time, most people send WeChat red packets or short messages to friends and relatives.

Setting Off Fireworks at Midnight

It has long been a Chinese tradition to set off **firecrackers** from the first minute of their new year. From public displays in major cities to millions of private celebrations in China's rural areas, setting off firecrackers and fireworks is an important activity.

Giving the Red Packets

The most common New Year gifts are red **packets**. Red packets have money in, and are believed to bring good luck because they are red. They are given to children and **retirees**. Customarily only employers give red packets to working adults.

1. Translate the following customs into Chinese.

Preparing for Chinese New Year_____

Having the reunion dinner_____

Staying up for midnight_____

Setting off fireworks at midnight_____

Giving the red envelopes_____

2. Draw a mind-map of celebrating the Spring Festival.

3. Complete your group's speech draft.

Topic：Chinese New Year

轻松一刻 The more you share, the happier you will be.

Chinese New Year's History and Its Evolution

The festival has a history of over 3,000 years. Celebrations on lunar New Year's Day can be dated back to the ancient **worship**（崇拜）of heaven and earth. Over the centuries new **traditions**（传统）were added and celebrations became more entertainment-orientated. It is still important to decorate their clean rooms featuring an **atmosphere**（气氛）of celebrations.

The Chinese character "福" (fu) is a must. The character written on paper can be **pasted**（粘贴）normally or upside down. In Chinese the reversed "福" (fu) is homophonic（谐音）with "fu comes", both being pronounced as "fudaole". What's more, two big red lanterns can be raised on both sides of the front door. Red **couplet**s（对联）can be pasted on doors. Red paper-cuttings can be seen on window glass and brightly colored New Year paintings with auspicious meanings may be put on the wall.

3-3　正月元宵闹一闹 The Lantern Festival

中文导读

　　元宵节,又称上元节、小正月、元夕或灯节,是春节之后的第一个重要节日,是中国亦是汉字文化圈的其他地区和海外华人的传统节日之一。正月是农历的元月,古人称夜为"宵",所以把一年中第一个月圆之夜正月十五称为元宵节。

　　中国古俗中将上元节(天官节、元宵节)、中元节(地官节、盂兰盆节)、下元节(水官节)合称"三元"。元宵节始于2000多年前的汉朝。汉文帝时下令将正月十五定为元宵节。汉武帝时,"太一神"(主宰宇宙一切之神)祭祀活动定在正月十五。司马迁创建"太初历"时,元宵节就已确定为重大节日。

　　元宵节的传统习俗有出门赏月、燃灯放焰、喜猜灯谜、共吃元宵、拉兔子灯等。此外,不少地方的元宵节还增加了耍龙灯、耍狮子、踩高跷、划旱船、扭秧歌、打太平鼓等传统民俗表演。

　　2008年6月,元宵节入选第二批国家级非物质文化遗产名录。

十个必背 The more you learn, the more you know.

1. **lantern** ['læntərn] *n.* 灯笼;提灯

   The night lantern glowed softly in the darkness.

   晚上点亮的灯笼在黑暗中发出柔和的光。

2. **riddle** ['rɪdl] *n.* 谜语;粗筛;猜不透的难题,难解之谜

   Scientists claimed yesterday to have solved the riddle of the birth of the universe.

   科学家们昨天声称已经解开了宇宙形成之谜。

3. **demonstrate** ['dɛmənˌstret] *v.* 论证;证明,证实;显示,展示;演示,说明

   The study also demonstrated a direct link between obesity and mortality.

   该研究还表明了肥胖症和死亡率之间存在直接的联系。

4. **smooth** [smuːð] *adj.* 光滑的;流畅的;柔软的;温和的,安详的

   The flagstones beneath their feet were worn smooth by centuries of use.

   他们脚下的石板路经过数百年的踩踏,被磨得光溜溜的。

5. **pull** [pʊl] *v.* 拉;拽;扯;拖

   Don't pull so hard or the handle will come off.

   别太使劲拉,不然把手会脱落。

6. outstanding [aʊtˈstændɪŋ] *adj.* 优秀的；杰出的

He's known to be an outstanding physicist.

他被公认为杰出的物理学家。

7. perform [pərˈfɔːrm] *v.* 表演

She performed a brief mime.

她表演了一小段哑剧。

8. ward [wɔːrd] *n.* 监护，守护；挡住，架住；避开；收容

A toddler was admitted to the emergency ward with a wound in his chest.

一个蹒跚学步的小孩因胸部受伤被送进急救室。

9. gong [ɡɔːŋ] *n.* 锣；钟状物；〈俚〉奖章，纪念章

On the stroke of seven, a gong summons guests into the dining-room.

7点整，一阵锣声将客人召集到餐厅。

10. glutinous [ˈɡlutnəs] *adj.* 黏的，胶质的

The sauce was glutinous and tasted artificial.

这种酱有些黏，尝起来不是非常地道。

三句必学 The more you practice, the more fluently you will speak.

1. Celebrated on the 15th day of the first lunar month, the **Lantern** Festival marks the end of the Spring Festival.

   元宵节是在农历正月十五这天庆祝的，它标志着春节的结束。

2. Lantern owners write **riddles** on paper notes and pasted them upon the colorful lanterns.

   灯笼的主人把谜语写在纸条上，再将纸条贴在五颜六色的灯笼上。

3. Lion dances are **performed** at important events to **ward** off evil and pray for good fortune and safety.

   舞狮是在重要的活动中进行的，以驱邪、祈祷好运和平安。

一篇必读 The more you read, the more knowledge you will get.

Celebrated on the 15th day of the first lunar month, the **Lantern** Festival marks the end of the Spring Festival. Lantern Festival activities vary regionally, including lighting and enjoying lanterns, guessing **riddles**, eating tangyuan (Yuanxiao) and so on.

Lighting and Watching Lanterns

Lanterns of various shapes and sizes can be seen. Children may hold small lanterns while walking the streets. The lanterns' artwork vividly **demonstrates** traditional Chinese images such as flowers, birds, people and buildings. Lighting lanterns is a way for people to pray for a **smooth** future and to express their best wishes for their families.

Guessing Lantern Riddles

Lantern owners write riddles on paper notes and pasted them upon the colorful lanterns. People can guess the riddles. If someone thinks they have the right answer, they can **pull** the riddle off and go to the lantern owner to check their answer. If the answer is right, there is usually a small gift as a prize.

Performing the Lion Dances

The lion dance is one of the most **outstanding** traditional folk dances in China. Lion dances are **performed** at important events to **ward** off evil and pray for good fortune and safety. The lion dance requires two highly-trained performers in a lion suit. One acts as the head and forelegs, and the other the back and rear legs. The "lion" dances to the beat of a drum, **gong**, and cymbals.

Eating Tangyuan

These ball-shaped dumplings are made of **glutinous** rice flour and are stuffed with different fillings such as white sugar, brown sugar, sesame seeds, peanuts or a combination of ingredients. They are usually sweet. Eating tangyuan on the Lantern Festival is a way for Chinese people to express their best wishes for their family and their future lives.

1. Translate the customs during the Lantern Festival.

Lighting and Watching Lanterns_____

Guessing Lantern Riddles_____

Performing the Lion Dances_____

Eating Tangyuan (Yuanxiao)_____

2. Draw a mind-map of celebrating the Lantern Festival.

3. Complete your group's speech draft.

Topic: The Lantern Festival

轻松一刻 **The more you share, the happier you will be.**

Cai Gaoqiao, or walking on **stilts**（高跷）, is another popular traditional performance of the Spring Festival, especially in Northern China. Cai means walking on and Gaoqiao means stilts. The ancient Chinese began using stilts to help them **gather**（收集）fruits from trees. This practical use of stilts gradually developed into a kind of folk dance. **Scholars**（学者）believe Gaoqiao originates from the totem worship of primitive clans and the fishermen's lives along the **coast**（海岸）.

Gaoqiao performance requires a high degree of skill and has various forms. Usually performers tie two long stilts to their feet, making them higher than others when standing on stilts. Most stilts are made of wood. There are "double stilts" and "single stilt" performances. Gaoqiao has now **assumed**（呈现）strong local **flavor**（风味）and national color.

3-4　端午佳节赛一赛Dragon Boat Festival

中文导读

　　端午节,日期为每年农历五月初五。据《荆楚岁时记》记载,因仲夏登高,顺阳在上,五月是仲夏,它的第一个午日正是登高顺阳好天气之日,故五月初五称为"端阳节"。此外,端午节还称午日节、五月节、龙舟节、浴兰节、诗人节等。端午节是流行于中国以及汉字文化圈其他诸国的传统文化节日。

　　端午节起源于中国,是古代吴越地区(长江中下游及以南一带)崇拜龙图腾的部族举行图腾祭祀的节日,有在农历五月初五以龙舟竞渡形式举行部落图腾祭祀的习俗之说。战国时期的楚国诗人屈原在该日抱石跳汨罗江自尽,百姓爱戴这位诗人便将端午作为纪念屈原的节日;部分地区也有纪念伍子胥、曹娥等说法。

　　端午节与春节、清明节、中秋节并称为中国民间的四大传统节日。自古以来端午节便有划龙舟及食粽等节日习俗。自2008年起,端午节被列为国家法定节假日。2006年5月,国务院将其列入首批国家级非物质文化遗产名录;2009年9月,联合国教科文组织正式审议并批准中国端午节列入世界非物质文化遗产名录,端午节也成为中国首个入选世界非遗的节日。

十个必背The more you learn, the more you know.

1. **dispel** [dɪˈspel] *v.* 打消;驱散;消除;驱散术;云散

   His speech dispelled any fears about his health.

   他的发言消除了人们对他身体健康的担心。

2. **invoke** [ɪnˈvoʊk] *v.* 乞灵于,祈求;祈祷;提出或授引……以支持或证明;召鬼;借助

   The judge invoked an international law that protects refugees.

   法官援引了一项保护难民的国际法。

3. **paddle** [ˈpædl] *v.* 用桨划动,用船桨推动(船只);搬运,运输;拍打;搅拌

   We might be able to push ourselves across with the paddle.

   我们也许可以用桨把自己推过去。

4. **accompany** [əˈkʌmpəni] *vt.* 陪同;陪伴;伴随;与……同时发生

   Accompanied by cheerful music, we began to dance.

   我们伴随着欢乐的乐曲跳起舞来。

5. **triangle** [ˈtraɪˌæŋgəl] *n.* 三角形;三人一组;三角铁;三角板

   This design is in pastel colors with three rectangles and three triangles.

这一设计由淡色的3个长方形和3个三角形构成。

6. **mosquito** [məˈski:toʊ] *n.* 蚊子

Are your mosquito bites still itching?

你被蚊子咬的地方还痒吗？

7. **aquatic** [əˈkwɑ:tɪk] *n.* 水产植物；*adj.* 水生；水生的；水栖的；水上的

The pond is quite small but can support many aquatic plants and fish.

池塘虽小，但能为许多水生植物和鱼类提供足够的养分。

8. **lintel** [ˈlɪntl] *n.* 楣，过梁

The door was so low that I hit my head on the lintel.

门太低，我的头都撞在了过梁上。

9. **alcoholic** [ˌælkəˈhɔ:lɪk] *adj.* 酒精的，含酒精的；酒精中毒的

He showed great courage by admitting that he is an alcoholic.

他以极大的勇气承认自己酗酒。

10. **perfume** [pərˈfju:m] *n.* 香水；香料；香味，香气

The hall smelled of her mother's perfume.

大厅里弥漫着她母亲身上的香水味。

三句必学 The more you practice, the more fluently you will speak.

1. It is a folk festival celebrated for over 2,000 years, when Chinese people practice various customs thought to **dispel** disease, and **invoke** good health.

这是一个庆祝了两千多年的民间节日，中国人在这个节日里有着各种各样的习俗，以驱除疾病，祈求健康。

2. Zongzi is wrapped in **triangle** or rectangle shapes in bamboo or reed leaves, and tied with soaked stalks or colorful silky cords.

粽子用粽叶或芦苇叶包裹成三角形或长方形，并用浸泡过的麻或彩色丝线捆扎。

3. During Dragon Boat Festival **perfume** pouches are hung around kids' necks or tied to the front of a garment as an ornament.

在端午节那天，香囊作为一个装饰品挂在孩子的脖子上或外衣上。

一篇必读 The more you read, the more knowledge you will get.

Dragon Boat Festival is a traditional festival full of traditions and superstitions. It is a folk festival celebrated for over 2,000 years, when Chinese people practice various customs thought to **dispel** disease, and **invoke** good health. Now many of the customs are disappearing. You are more likely to find them practiced in rural areas.

Holding Dragon Boat Racing

Dragon boat racing is the most important activity. The wooden boats are shaped and decorated in the form of a Chinese dragon. Generally it is about 20–35 meters in length and needs 30–60 people to **paddle** it. During the races, dragon boat teams paddle harmoniously and hurriedly, **accompanied** by the sound of beating drums.

Eating Sticky Rice Dumplings

Zongzi is wrapped in **triangle** or rectangle shapes in bamboo or reed leaves, and tied with soaked stalks or colorful silky cords. They are a kind of sticky rice dumplings made of glutinous rice filled with meats, beans, and other fillings.

Hanging Chinese Mugwort and Calamus

The fragrance of Mugwort is very pleasant, deterring flies and **mosquitoes.** Calamus is an **aquatic** plant that has similar effects. On the fifth day of the fifth month, people usually hang mugwort and calamus on doors **lintels** to discourage diseases.

Drinking Realgar Wine

Realgar wine is a Chinese **alcoholic** drink consisting of fermented cereals and powdered realgar. There is an old saying: "Drinking realgar wine drives diseases and evils away!"

Wearing Perfume Pouches

During Dragon Boat Festival perfume pouches are hung around kids' necks or tied to the front of a garment as an ornament. The perfume pouches are said to protect them from evils.

1. Translate the customs during Dragon Boat Festival.

Holding Dragon Boat Racing _____

Eating Sticky Rice Dumplings_____

Hanging Chinese Mugwort and Calamus_____

Drinking Realgar Wine_____

Wearing Perfume Pouches_____

2. Draw something about the Dragon Boat Festival.

3. Complete your group's speech draft.

Topic：Dragon Boat Festival

轻松一刻 **The more you share, the happier you will be.**

How Did Dragon Boat Festival Start

There are many **legends**（传说）about the origin of the Dragon Boat Festival. The most popular one is in **commemoration**（纪念）of Qu Yuan. **Qu Yuan**（340–278 BC）was a **patriotic**（爱国的）poet and **exiled** （放逐）official during the Warring States Period of ancient China. He **drowned**（使淹死）himself in the Miluo River on the 5th day of the 5th Chinese lunar month, when his beloved Chu State fell to the State of Qin. Local people desperately tried to save Qu Yuan and recover his body.

In order to commemorate Qu Yuan, every fifth day of the fifth lunar month people beat drums and paddle out in boats on the river as they once did to keep fish and evil spirits away from his body.

3-5　中秋佳节圆一圆 Mid-Autumn Festival

中文导读

　　中秋节,又称月夕、秋节、仲秋节、八月节、八月会、追月节、玩月节、拜月节、女儿节或团圆节,是流行于中国众多民族与汉字文化圈诸国的传统文化节日,时在农历八月十五。因其恰值三秋之半,故名,也有些地方将中秋节定在八月十六。

　　中秋节始于唐朝初年,盛行于宋朝,至明清时,已成为与春节齐名的中国传统节日之一。受中华文化的影响,中秋节也是东亚和东南亚一些国家尤其是当地的华人华侨的传统节日。2008年,中秋节被列为国家法定节假日。2006年5月20日,国务院将其列入首批国家级非物质文化遗产名录。

　　中秋节自古便有祭月、赏月、拜月、吃月饼、赏桂花、饮桂花酒等习俗,流传至今。中秋节以月之圆兆人之团圆,寄托思念故乡和亲人之情,祈盼丰收、幸福,成为丰富多彩、弥足珍贵的文化遗产。中秋节与端午节、春节、清明节并称为中国四大传统节日。

十个必背 The more you learn, the more you know.

1. **derive** [dɪˈraɪv] *v.* 得到;(从⋯⋯中)提取

Many English words are derived from Latin and Greek words.

许多英语词是从拉丁词和希腊词中派生而来的。

2. **worship** [ˈwɜːrʃɪp] *n.* 崇拜;敬仰;礼拜

Therefore, Chinese attitudes towards nature are Nature Worship and Embrace the Nature.

中国人对自然的态度是崇敬自然、拥抱自然。

3. **dynasty** [ˈdaɪnəsti] *n.* 王朝;朝代

The Seljuk dynasty of Syria was founded in 1094.

叙利亚的塞尔柱王朝始建于1094年。

4. **harvest** [ˈhɑːrvɪst] *n.* 收割;收成;收获季节;结果

There were about 300 million tons of grain in the fields at the start of the harvest.

收获伊始,地里大概有3亿吨粮食。

5. **reunion** [riˈjunjən] *n.* 重聚,(亲友等的)聚会;再结合,再合并;再统一

The Association holds an annual reunion.

这个协会每年聚会一次。

6. crab [kræb] *n.* 蟹,蟹肉;脾气乖戾的人;[植]沙果,沙果树

Thousands of herring and crab are washed up on the beaches during every storm.

每次暴风雨过后海滩上都会留下数不尽的鲱鱼和螃蟹。

7. pumpkin ['pʌmpkɪn] *n.* 南瓜

Quarter the pumpkin and remove the seeds.

将南瓜切成4份,去掉籽。

8. pomelo ['pɑ:məloʊ] *n.* 柚子

Botanists believe that crosses between pomelo and wild orange created grapefruit.

植物学家相信柚子和野生桔子的杂交产生了葡萄柚。

9. nutritious [nu'trɪʃəs] *adj.* 有营养的,滋养的

It is always important to choose enjoyable, nutritious foods.

选择好吃的、营养价值高的食物总是很重要。

10. prefer [prɪ'fɚ] *v.* 更喜欢;提升,提拔;给予(债权人)优先权;提出(控告)

Does he prefer a particular sort of music?

他有特别喜欢的音乐吗?

三句必学 The more you practice, the more fluently you will speak.

1. Mid-Autumn Festival is a **harvest** festival.

中秋节是一个丰收的节日。

2. It means family **reunion** and peace.

它意味着家庭团聚与和平。

3. Mooncakes are the must-eat Mid-Autumn food in China.

月饼是中国人中秋必吃的食品。

一篇必读 The more you read, the more knowledge you will get.

The festival has history of over 3,000 years. It was **derived** from the custom of moon **worship** during the Shang **Dynasty** (1600-1046 BC). It was first celebrated as a festival during the Northern Song Dynasty (960-1127). Like the emperors, ancient people believed worshiping the moon and eating together round a table would bring them good luck and happiness.

Mid-Autumn Festival is a **harvest** festival. It takes places on August 15th in Chinese lunar calendar. This festival means family **reunion** and peace. It is celebrated when the moon is believed to be the biggest and fullest.

Chinese people celebrate the festival with many traditional and meaningful activities. Mooncakes are the must-eat Mid-Autumn food in China. Chinese people see in the roundness of mooncakes a symbol of reunion and happiness. Other foods eaten during the festival are harvest foods, such as **crab**s, **pumpkins**, **pomelo**s, and grapes. People enjoy them at their freshest and most **nutritious**.

Since 2008, the festival has been a 3-day public holiday in mainland China. New celebrations have developed in recent years. The younger generations **prefer** traveling, surfing the Internet, and using smart phone apps to celebrate with their families.

1. Fill in the blanks.

Mid-Autumn Festival is a _____ festival. It takes places on August the 15th of the Chinese _____. It means family _____ and peace. It is _____ when the moon is believed to be the biggest and _____.

2. Draw the food people will eat on the Mid-Autumn Festival.

3. Complete your group's speech draft.

Topic：Mid-Autumn Festival in China

轻松一刻 The more you share, the happier you will be.

How Mid-Autumn Is Celebrated in China's Neighboring Countries

In many of China's neighboring nations, Mid-Autumn is widely celebrated. Many interesting activities with unique local features are held.

In **Singapore**（新加坡）, **Malaysia**（马来西亚）, and the **Philippines**（菲律宾）, countries with many **ethnic**（民族的）Chinese citizens, celebrations are more Chinese, such as lighting lanterns and dragon dances.

In other countries, such as Japan and **Vietnam**（越南）, which have also been influenced deeply by Chinese culture, new celebrations have been derived from their unique cultures.

Tea in Chinese Culture

4-1　饮茶历史讲一讲 Chinese Tea Culture

中文导读

　　中国人饮茶,注重一个"品"字。"品茶"不但可以鉴别茶的优劣,也带有神思遐想和领略饮茶情趣之意。在百忙之中泡上一壶浓茶,择雅静之处,自斟自饮,可以消除疲劳、涤烦益思、振奋精神,也可以细啜慢饮,达到美的享受,使精神世界升华到高尚的艺术境界。品茶的环境一般由建筑物、园林、摆设等因素组成。饮茶要求安静、清新、舒适、干净的环境。中国园林世界闻名,山水风景更是不可胜数。在园林或自然山水,用木头做亭子、凳子,搭设茶室,诗情画意、意趣盎然。

　　中国是文明古国、礼仪之邦,很重礼节。但凡来了客人,沏茶、敬茶的礼仪是必不可少的。当有客来访的,可征求意见,选用最合来客口味和最佳茶具待客。以茶敬客时,对茶叶适当拼配也是必要的。主人在陪伴客人饮茶时,要注意客人杯、壶中的茶水有余量,一般用茶杯泡茶,如客人已喝去一半,就要添加开水,随喝随添,使茶水浓度基本保持前后一致,水温适宜。在饮茶时也可适当佐以茶食、糖果、菜肴等。

　　中国茶文化的内容主要是茶在中国精神文化中的体现,比"茶风俗""茶道"的范畴深广得多,这也是中国茶文化之所以与欧美或日本的茶文化区别很大的原因。

十个必背 The more you learn, the more you know.

1. accidental [ˌæksɪˈdentl] *adj.* 意外的;偶然的

He can face the accidental trouble.

他能够面对意外的困难。

2. boil [bɔɪl] *v.* 煮;煮沸;(使)沸腾;(把壶、锅等)里面的水烧开

Heat the cream to boiling point and pour three quarters of it over the chocolate.

把奶油煮沸,然后把其中的3/4浇到巧克力上。

3. distant [ˈdɪstənt] *adj.* 遥远的;远处的

He used to work in a distant land.

他曾在一个遥远的国度工作。

4. bush [bʊʃ] *n.* 灌木

There was someone skulking behind the bushes.

有人藏在灌木后面。

5. refreshing [rɪ'freʃ] *v.* 刷新;使恢复精力

Click here to refresh this document.

点击此处以刷新文件。

6. legend ['ledʒənd] *n.* 传奇;传说;传奇故事

He was a colossus, a legend.

他是一个伟人,一个传奇人物。

7. gradual ['grædʒuəl] *adj.* 逐渐的;渐进的;逐步的

Losing weight is a slow, gradual process.

减肥是一个缓慢而渐进的过程。

8. manufacture [ˌmænju'fæktʃər] *vt.* 制造;(用机器)大量生产

A big factory manufactures goods in large quantities by using machines.

大工厂使用机器大量制造商品。

9. economic [ˌiːkə'nɑːmɪk] *adj.* 经济的;经济上的

Our future prosperity depends on economic growth.

我们未来的繁荣昌盛依赖经济的发展。

10. national ['næʃnəl] *adj.* 国家的;民族的

Class sizes in the school are below the national average.

这所学校班上的人数少于全国平均数。

三句必学 The more you practice, the more fluently you will speak.

1. Did you know that tea, the most popular drink in the world (after water), was an **accidental** invention?
   你知道世界上最受欢迎的饮料茶(仅次于水)是偶然出现的吗?
2. Dried leaves from a nearby bush fell into the **boiling** water and it generated a nice smell.
   附近灌木丛里的干树叶掉进沸水里,发出一股好闻的气味。
3. The tea trade from China to Western countries took place in the 19th century.
   从中国到西方国家的茶叶贸易发生在19世纪。

一篇必读 The more you read, the more knowledge you will get.

Did you know that tea, the most popular drink in the world (after water), was an **accidental** invention? Many people believe that tea was first appeared in about 5,000 years ago. It is said that a Chinese ruler Shen Nong was the first to discover tea as a drink.

A story goes that, Shen Nong is said to have lived 5,000 years ago and he required that all drinking water to be **boiled**. One summer day, while visiting a **distant** part of his realm, he and his court stopped to rest. The servants began to boil water for them to drink. Dried leaves from a nearby **bush** fell into the boiling water and it generated a nice smell. Shen Nong was interested in the brown water and tasted it. He found it very **refreshing**. Therefore, according to **legend**, tea was created in 2737 BC.

The history of Chinese tea is a long and **gradual** story. Generations of growers and producers have perfected the Chinese way of **manufacturing** tea. Tea is an important part of Chinese tradition. As Chinese society developed, tea production has played a role in driving **economic** development.

It is believed that tea was brought to Korea and Japan during the 6th and 7th centuries. Tea did not appear until around 1660 in England, but it had become the **national** drink in less than 100 years. The tea **trade** from China to Western countries took place in the 19th century. This helped to spread the popularity of tea and the tea plant to more places around the world. Even though many people now know about tea culture, Chinese are without doubt the ones who understand the nature of tea best.

1. Describe the story of Shen Nong and tea.

A story goes that, Shen Nong _____. One summer day, while visiting a **distant** part of his realm, he and the court stopped to rest. The servants began to boil water for them to drink. _____ . Shen Nong was interested in the brown water and tasted it. _____. And so, according to **legend**, tea was created in 2737 BC.

2. Fill in the blanks.

The history of Chinese tea is a long and_____ story. _____ of growers and producers have perfected the Chinese way of _____ tea. Tea is an important part of Chinese tradition. As Chinese society _____, tea production has played a role in driving _____ development.

3. Complete your group's speech draft.

Topic：Chinese Tea Culture

轻松一刻 **The more you share, the happier you will be.**

Drinking tea offers **numerous**（很多的）benefits. It refreshes the mind, clears heat within the human body and helps people lose weight. As you add a cup of tea to your daily routine, please check the following tips, which help you reap the maximum health benefits.

1. Drink it hot. Tea **oxidizes**（氧化）quickly after brewing, and its nutrients diminish overtime.

2. Do not drink too much strong tea. It is likely to upset your stomach and cause **insomnia**（失眠症）if you make the tea too strong.

3. The best time to drink is between meals. If you drink tea soon after or before meals, it may **quench**（解渴）appetite when your stomach is empty, or cause indigestion when your stomach is full.

4. Do not drink with medication. Tea contains large amount of tannin, which will react with certain elements in the medicine, thus reduce medical effects.

5. Green tea is the best option for office workers. Green tea contains **catechins**（茶多酚）that help prevent computer radiation.

4-2　茗茶趣事聊一聊 Interesting Facts about Tea

中文导读

中国是茶的故乡。中国人饮茶,据说始于神农时代,少说也有4700多年了。直到现在,中国各族同胞还有以茶代礼的风俗。

中国人对茶的配制是多种多样的:有太湖的熏豆茶、苏州的香味茶、湖南的姜盐茶、成都的盖碗茶、台湾的冻顶茶、杭州的龙井茶、福建的乌龙茶等。

种茶、饮茶不等于有了茶文化,仅是茶文化形成的前提条件,还必须有文人的参与和文化的内涵。唐代陆羽所著《茶经》系统地总结了唐代以及唐以前茶叶生产、饮用的经验,提出了精行俭德的茶道精神。陆羽和皎然等一批文化人非常重视茶的精神享受和道德规范,讲究饮茶用具、饮茶用水和煮茶艺术,并与儒、道、佛哲学思想交融。一些士大夫和文人雅士在饮茶过程中,还创作了很多茶诗,仅在《全唐诗》中,流传至今的就有百余位诗人的四百余首,由此奠定了中国茶文化的基础。茶叶,令中国茶坛大放异彩。

中国茶文化是中国制茶、饮茶的文化。作为"开门七件事"(柴米油盐酱醋茶)之一,饮茶在中国古代是非常普遍的。中国的茶文化与欧美或日本的茶文化有很大的区别。中华茶文化源远流长,博大精深,不但包含物质文化层面,还彰显深厚的精神文明层次。《茶经》在历史上吹响了中华茶文化的号角。从此,茶的精神渗透到宫廷和社会,深入中国的诗词、绘画、书法、宗教、医学。几千年来,中国不但积累了大量关于茶叶种植、生产的物质文化,更积累了丰富的有关茶的精神文化,这就是中国特有的茶文化,其属于文化学范畴。

十个必背 The more you learn, the more you know.

1. evolve [ɪˈvɒlv] *v.* 演变,进化;(动植物等)进化,进化形成

This was when he evolved the working method from which he has never departed.

就在这个时候,他逐步形成了那种他一直沿用至今的工作方法。

2. beverage [ˈbɛvərɪdʒ] *n.* 饮料

Alcoholic beverages are served in the hotel lounge.

酒店的公共休息室出售酒精饮料。

3. integral [ˈɪntɪɡrəl] *adj.* 完整的;不可或缺的;必需的

Community involvement is now integral to company strategy.

参与社会活动如今已是公司战略中必不可少的内容。

4. consumed [kən'suːmd] *v.* 消耗,耗费;吃;喝;饮(consume 的过去式和过去分词)

No alcohol may be consumed on the premises.

场区内禁止饮酒。

5. primarily [praɪ'mɛrəli] *v.* 首先;首要地,主要地;根本上;本来

Public order is primarily an urban problem.

社会治安主要是城市的问题。

6. infusion [ɪn'fjuːʒn] *n.* 灌输;注入;沏成的饮料

Make an infusion by boiling and simmering the rhubarb and camomile together.

将大黄和甘菊一起煮沸再用文火炖,熬成汤药。

7. export ['ekspɔːrt] *v.* 出口,输出

The nation also exports beef.

该国也出口牛肉。

8. merchant ['mɜːrtʃənt] *n.* 商人;批发商

Venice was once a city of rich merchants.

威尼斯曾是富商云集的城市。

9. region ['riːdʒən] *n.* 地区

Nowadays tractors are used even in remote mountainous regions.

现在连偏僻的山区也用上了拖拉机。

10. finicky ['fɪnɪki] *adj.* 挑剔的;(对衣食等)过分讲究的

It's a very finicky job.

这是个很细致的工作。

三句必学 The more you practice, the more fluently you will speak.

1. Then it **evolved** into a type of **beverage** and became an integral part of Chinese culture.
   后来它演变成一种饮料,成为中国文化不可分割的一部分。

2. Tea is the national drink in China, but the production and consumption of tea is distinctive in different **regions**.
   茶是中国的民族饮品,但不同地区的茶叶生产和消费各不相同。

3. Chinese people are usually really **finicky** about the teaware they use for brewing or drinking tea.
   中国人通常对他们用来泡茶或喝茶的茶具非常挑剔。

一篇必读 The more you read, the more knowledge you will get.

Tea was first discovered by the Chinese and used as medicine. Later, it **evolved** into a type of **beverage** and became an **integral** part of Chinese culture. Here are some interesting facts about Chinese tea to help you learn more about it.

Tea is the Second Most Consumed Beverage in China.

Nowadays, tea is **consumed** around the world more than any other beverage except for water. You can find lots of teahouses in China easily, especially in the top tea culture cities.

Tea Was First Used as Medicine.

Before the 8th century BC, tea in China was **primarily** used as a medicine. Ancient Chinese people often boiled fresh tea leaves and drank the **infusion.** They believed that tea reduced "heat" and improved eyesight.

Tea is China's Oldest Exported Product.

China was the first exporter of tea. Near the end of the Ming Dynasty (1368–1644 AD), British **merchants** set up trading posts in Xiamen, Fujian Province and first started to trade in Chinese tea.

Tea Grown in Different Areas Has Different Flavors.

Tea is the national drink in China, but the production and consumption of tea is distinctive in different **regions**. On the one hand, different regions are famous for growing different types of tea. On the other hand, people in different regions tend to prefer drinking different teas.

Serving Tea to Elders or Guests Is A Sign of Respect.

In traditional Chinese culture, serving tea to a guest is a sign of respect. A younger person can show respect and **gratitude** to an older person by offering a cup of tea. This is especially common during big celebrations, such as birthdays, the Spring Festival or a traditional Chinese wedding.

Chinese People Think A Tea Set Is Very Important for A Good Cup of Tea.

Chinese people are usually really **finicky** about the teaware they use for brewing or drinking tea. They believe that different tea sets affect the tea's flavor. The most popular teapot in China is the Yixing (a city in the eastern Chinese province of Jiangsu) clay teapot.

1. Translate some interesting facts about Chinese tea.

Chinese people think a tea set is very important for a good cup of tea.

_____

Serving tea to elders or guests is a sign of respect.

_____

Tea grown in different areas has different flavors.

_____

Tea is China's oldest exported product.

_____

2. Fill in the blanks.

Tea was first discovered by the Chinese and used as_____. Then it evolved into a type of _____ and became an _____ part of Chinese culture. There are some interesting _____ about Chinese tea to help you learn more about it. For example, tea is the second most consumed _____ in China.

3. Complete your group's speech draft.

Topic：Interesting Things about Chinese Tea

轻松一刻 The more you share, the happier you will be.

Tea is a great "**social**（社会的）media" in China. A teahouse is the by-product of Chinese tea culture. A Chinese tea house refers to the public place where people gather to drink tea and generally developed into a public **entertainment**（娱乐）place as well.

Chinese tea house has a long history. It first formed during the Tang dynasty Kaiyuan era（713—714）and became popular during the Song Dynasty. From the Ming and Qing dynasties, tea house culture was integrated with regional culture.

Chinese people generally consider meeting in a teahouse to be a good **opportunity**（机会）to **socialize**（社交）or discuss business matters. Chinese scholars prefer to have free and deep communication with their friends.

4-3　知名绿茶品一品 Popular Green Tea

中文导读

　　绿茶,中国的主要茶类之一,是指采取茶树的新叶或芽,未经发酵,经杀青、整形、烘干等工艺制作而成的茶。其制成品的色泽和冲泡后的茶汤较多地保存了鲜茶叶的绿色格调。常饮绿茶能防癌、降脂和减肥。吸烟者常饮绿茶也可减轻其受到的尼古丁伤害。

　　绿茶由于未经发酵,保留了鲜叶的天然物质,含有的茶多酚、儿茶素、叶绿素、咖啡碱、氨基酸、维生素等,营养成分也较多。绿茶中的这些天然营养成分能防衰老、防癌、抗癌、杀菌、消炎等。绿茶是以适宜茶树新梢为原料,经杀青、揉捻、干燥等典型工艺过程制成的茶叶。其干茶色泽和冲泡后的茶汤、叶底以绿色为主调,故名绿茶。绿茶是将采摘来的鲜叶先经高温杀青,杀灭了各种氧化酶,保持了茶叶的绿色,然后经揉捻、干燥而制成,清汤绿叶是绿茶品质的共同特点。中国生产绿茶的范围极为广泛,河南、贵州、江西、安徽、浙江、江苏、四川、陕西(陕南)、湖南、湖北、广西、福建是我国的绿茶主产省份。

十个必背 The more you learn, the more you know.

1. **essential** [ɪˈsɛnʃəl] *adj.* 必要的;本质的;基本的;精华的

   It was absolutely essential to separate crops from the areas that animals used as pasture.

   将庄稼和放牧区分开绝对必要。

2. **millennium** [məˈlɛniəm] *adj.* 千禧年;一千年;千年期;全人类未来的幸福时代

   Acupuncture was practiced in China as long ago as the third millennium BC.

   中国早在公元前3000年就已开始采用针灸疗法。

3. **reputation** [ˌrɛpjuˈteʃən] *n.* 名气,名声;好名声;信誉,声望;荣誉,名望

   Alice Munro has a reputation for being a very depressing writer.

   艾丽斯·芒罗以文风沉郁闻名。

4. **peak** [piːk] *n.* 峰;高峰;顶峰;山峰

   We are far from reaching the peak.

   我们还远未达到顶峰。

5. **fragrant** [ˈfreɪɡrənt] *adj.* 芳香的;香的

   The flowers gave off a fragrant perfume.

   花儿散发出芳香。

6. lingering[ˈlɪŋɡərɪŋ] *adj.* 逗留(linger的现在分词);缓慢消失;苟延残喘;持续看(或思考)

He would rather be killed in a race than die a lingering death in hospital.

他宁肯在比赛中丢了性命也不愿在医院里苟延残喘。

7. literally[ˈlɪtərəli] *adj.* 逐字地;照字面地;确实地,真正地;[口]差不多,简直(用于加强语意)

We've got to get the economy under control or it will literally eat us up.

我们必须设法控制经济,不然它非把我们吞噬了不可。

8. imperial[ɪmˈpɪriəl] *adj.* 帝国的,皇帝的;皇家的,庄严的;特级的;度量衡英制的

They executed Russia's imperial family in 1918.

他们在1918年处死了俄国沙皇皇族。

9. luster[ˈlʌstɚ] *n.* 光泽;光彩;光辉;荣耀

The chair has a metallic luster.

这把椅子有金属光泽。

10. delicate[ˈdɛlɪkɪt] *adj.* 微妙的;熟练的;纤弱的;易损的

He had delicate hands.

他有一双纤细的手。

三句必学 The more you practice, the more fluently you will speak.

1. It enjoys a high **reputation** for the sake of its gentle flavor and pleasing aroma.

   它以其温和的风味和令人愉悦的香气而享有盛誉。

2. It is cropped during the spring equinox and grain rain period, and it has a curled shape resembling a snail.

   它是在春分和谷雨期间种植的,它有一个类似蜗牛的卷曲形状。

3. Listed as a tribute tea in the Song Dynasty (960-1279), Yunwu ("cloud mist") tea is grown on Lushan Mountain, Jiangxi Province.

   作为宋朝贡品茶(960—1279),"云雾"产于江西省的庐山。

一篇必读 The more you read, the more knowledge you will get.

Tea is one of the **essential** parts of Chinese people's lives. The custom of drinking tea dates back to the third **millennium** BC in China and green tea is the most popular type of tea there. Here are eight high-quality teas with a high **reputation** in China. Most of the teas are named after their original producing areas.

West Lake Dragon Well Tea（西湖龙井）

Producing area: West Lake area in Hangzhou

Dragon Well tea, also known as Longjing tea, is the most famous green tea in China and is famous around the world. Its gentle flavor and pleasing **aroma** enjoy a high reputation.

Biluochun（碧螺春）

Producing area: Dongting Mountain, Suzhou

It is cropped during the spring equinox and "grain rain" period, and it has a curled shape resembling a snail. It has a strong aroma and fruity taste.

Huangshan Maofeng Tea（黄山毛峰）

Producing area: Huizhou City, Anhui

It's picked in the early spring. It has **peak**-shaped leaves with ivory-tinted hairs, and its golden tea is slightly sweet and **fragrant** with a **lingering** aftertaste.

Taiping Houkui Tea（太平猴魁）

Producing area: Yellow Mountain, Anhui

Taiping houkui **literally** means "monkey leader" in Taiping Prefecture (the Huangshan area). It has a straight shape just like a bamboo leaf, which is rare among tea and its leaves are larger than other types.

Lu'an Melon Seed Tea（六安瓜片）

Producing area: Lu'an City, Anhui

Lu'an Melon Seed tea was a type of tribute tea for the **imperial** family during the Qing Dynasty. It was widely used to prevent sunstroke by the Chinese during the Ming Dynasty (1368-1644).

Xinyang Maojian Tea（信阳毛尖）

Producing area: Xinyang City, Henan Province

Maojian ("hairy tips") is a special type of tea. Compared to other types of tea, Xinyang Maojian leaves are relatively small, with a green color and white hairs.

Lushan Yunwu Tea（庐山云雾）

Producing area: Lushan, JiuJiang City, Jiangxi Province

Listed as a tribute tea in the Song Dynasty (960-1279), Yunwu ("cloud mist") tea is grown on Lushan Mountain, Jiangxi Province. It's characterized by its tender leaves, jade green **luster**, clear tea and sweet flavor.

Nanjing Rain Flower Tea（南京雨花茶）

Producing area: Yuhuatai District, Nanjing, Jiangsu Province

Nanjing Rain Flower tea leaves are processed with great care and have a **delicate** appearance with a pine needle shape. It has a light, smooth, and sweet flowery taste.

1. Describe each popular type of tea in one sentence.

eg. The West Lake Dragon Well Tea enjoys a high reputation for its gentle flavor and pleasing aroma.

_____

_____

2. Guess which tea it is.

It has a straight shape just like a bamboo leaf which is rare among tea and its leaves are larger than other types.	
The tea leaves are processed with great care and have a delicate appearance with a pine needle shape.	

续表

It has **peak**-shaped leaves with ivory-tinted hairs, and its golden tea is slightly sweet and **fragrant** with a **lingering** aftertaste.	
It has a curled shape resembling a snail. It has a strong aroma and fruity taste.	

3. Complete your group's speech draft.

Topic：Green Tea

轻松一刻 **The more you share, the happier you will be.**

How to Make a Perfect Cup of Longjing Tea

Preparation（准备工作）. Get some Longjing tea, a glass cup, and a bottle of **mineral**（矿物）spring water ready, and then put three grams（one teaspoon）of tea into the cup.

Clean the tea leaves. Pour a little（about 50 ml）heated spring water（80°C to 90°C）into the cup. Gently **swirl** the cup, and then pour out the water, keeping the tea leaves in the cup. This should clean off any dust etc. on the tea from the manufacturing process.

Brew the tea. Pour 150 ml of 85°C water in to the cup, and wait for seven minutes until the tea leaves have **dilated**（扩大展开）owing to the **absorption**（吸收）of the water.

Drink the Tea: Drink the tea in the following three minutes, and you can enjoy a perfect cup of Longjing tea.

4-4　西湖龙井饮一饮 West Lake Dragon Well Tea

中文导读

　　西湖龙井,属绿茶,中国十大名茶之一,产于浙江省杭州市西湖龙井村周围群山,并因此得名,具有1200多年历史。清乾隆游览杭州西湖时,盛赞西湖龙井茶,把狮峰山下胡公庙前的十八棵茶树封为"御茶"。西湖龙井按外形和内质的优次分作1—8级。

　　特级西湖龙井茶扁平光滑挺直,色泽嫩绿光润,香气鲜嫩清高,滋味鲜爽甘醇,叶底细嫩呈朵。清明节前采制的龙井茶简称明前龙井,美称女儿红,"院外风荷西子笑,明前龙井女儿红"。西湖龙井茶与西湖一样,是人、自然、文化三者的完美结晶,是西湖地域文化的重要载体。

十个必背 The more you learn, the more you know.

1. **mellow** ['meloʊ] *adj.* 圆润的;(瓜,果等)成熟的;(酒)芳醇的;(颜色或声音)柔和的

   His voice was deep and mellow and his speech had a soothing and comforting quality.

   他的嗓音低沉悦耳,他的讲话能抚慰人心。

2. **elaborate** [ɪ'læbəreɪt] *adj.* 精心制作的;精巧的;复杂的;(结构)复杂的

   He is known for his elaborate costumes.

   他以着装精致而闻名。

3. **timeliness** ['taimlinəs] *n.* 及时,时间性;时效性

   Timeliness is often more important than precision to managers.

   对管理者来说,信息的及时性经常比精密度更重要。

4. **grade** [greɪd] *n.* 等级;(产品、材料的)品级

   Milk is sold in grades.

   牛奶是分等级出售的。

5. **iron** ['aɪərn] *n.* 铁器,铁制品;熨斗,烙铁;坚强;脚镣

   The huge, iron gate was locked.

   巨大的铁门紧锁着。

6. **grasp** [græsp] *adj.* 抓住;了解;急忙抓住;急切(或贪婪)地抓住

   He grasped both my hands.

   他紧紧抓住我的双手。

7. **buckle** ['bʌkl] *vt.* 用搭扣扣紧;(使)变形,弯曲

He wore a belt with a large brass buckle.

他系着一条带大铜扣的腰带。

8. grind [graɪnd] *v.* 折磨;磨碎,嚼碎

Store the peppercorns in an airtight container and grind the pepper as you need it.

将胡椒粒储存在密封容器中,在需要的时候磨成粉。

9. rub [rʌb] *v.* 擦;磨;搓

I rubbed at the stain on the cloth.

我擦了擦布上的污渍。

10. moisture ['mɔɪstʃər] *n.* 潮湿;水分;水汽;潮气

The sun is constantly evaporating the earth's moisture.

太阳使地球上的湿气不断蒸发。

三句必学 The more you practice, the more fluently you will speak.

1. Longjing tea, also known as West Lake Dragon Well tea, has topped the list of the ten most famous teas in China and it is characterized by its green color, delicate aroma, **mellow** taste and beautiful shape.

   龙井茶,又称西湖龙井茶,以其色泽翠绿、香气细腻、口感醇厚、形状优美而居中国十大名茶之首。

2. The tea leaves picked before the Qingming Festival (Tomb-Sweeping Day) or after the "grain rain" period (6th solar term) are considered to be the top grade.

   清明节(清明节)前或"谷雨"期(第六个节气)后采摘的茶叶被视为上等茶叶。

3. A skillful tea-making master knows exactly how and when to use a certain technique according to the changes of **moisture** and temperature.

   一个熟练的制茶大师根据湿度和温度的变化准确地知道如何以及何时使用某种技术。

一篇必读 The more you read, the more knowledge you will get.

Longjing tea, also known as West Lake Dragon Well tea, has topped the list of the ten most famous teas in China and it is characterized by its green color, delicate aroma, **mellow** taste and beautiful shape. Both the picking and making processes of Longjing tea are **elaborate** in order to make sure it retains its high quality and original flavor.

The **timeliness** of picking leaves is very important. The tea leaves picked before the Qingming Festival (Tomb-Sweeping Day) or after the "grain rain" period (6th solar term) are considered to be the top **grade**.

The process of making Longjing tea is very strict. It usually employs **iron** pans for baking the tea and it involves ten techniques based on different temperatures and moisture, including shaking, **grasping**, **buckling**, pressing, **grinding**, **rubbing,** and throwing. A skillful tea-making master knows exactly how and when to use a certain technique according to the changes of **moisture** and temperature.

1. Fill in the blanks.

Longjing tea, also known as West Lake Dragon Well tea, has topped the _____ of the ten most famous teas in China and it is characterized by its _____ color, delicate _____, _____ taste and beautiful _____ . Both the _____ and _____ processes of Longjing tea are elaborate in order to make sure it retains its high _____ and original flavor.

2. Draw a mind-map of making West Lake Dragon Well Tea.

3. Complete your group's speech draft.

Topic：West Lake Dragon Well Tea

轻松一刻 **The more you share, the happier you will be.**

Legends of Longjing Tea—Admiration from the Imperial Family

The legend went that Emperor Qianlong visited Lion Peak Mountain during his Hangzhou travels, and he saw some ladies picking the tea at the foot of the mountain. He was so interested in their movements that he decided to have a go himself.

While picking the tea, he received the news of his mother's illness, so he carelessly put the leaves in his right **sleeve**（套筒）and left Hangzhou for Beijing. He visited his mother immediately upon his arrival in Beijing, and **Empress Dowager**（太后）smelt the fragrance of the leaves from his sleeves and wanted to have a taste.

Emperor Qianlong ordered some tea to be brewed for her, and she found herself completely refreshed after drinking a cup of tea. She even praised it as a **remedy**（药品）for all ills. From then on, Shi Feng Longjing tea was listed as the **tribute**（贡品）tea especially for Empress Dowager.

4-5 常见茶具见一见 Chinese Tea Sets

中文导读

"一器成名只为茗,悦来客满是茶香。"中国人自古喜饮茶、善饮茶,且饮茶多讲究,茶文化也普及,故茶具文化源远流长,种类繁多,造型优美,既有实用价值,又富艺术之美,故驰名中外,成为了历代爱茶人眼中至宝。

冲泡好一杯佳茗,配具也必不可少,犹如绿叶之于红花,彩云之于明月,有映衬之妙。古时痴迷茶艺的文人雅士,无不把茶具的选择搭配,放在极为重要的位置。苏东坡有"潞公煎茶学西蜀,定州花瓷琢玉红",范仲淹有"黄金碾畔玉尘飞,碧玉瓯中素涛起",茶具不仅具有实用功能,更有鉴赏把玩的趣味。

十个必背 The more you learn, the more you know.

1. attach [əˈtætʃ] *v.* 附上;贴上,系

We attach labels to things before we file them away.

存档前,我们先贴上标签。

2. pottery [ˈpɑːtəri] *n.* 陶器;陶器厂[作坊];[集合词]陶器类;陶器制造

Some bowls were made of pottery and wood.

一些碗是用陶土和木头制成的。

3. porcelain [ˈpɔːrsəlɪn] *n.* 瓷,瓷器

There were lilies everywhere in tall white porcelain vases.

高高的白色瓷瓶上绘满了百合花。

4. lacquer [ˈlækə] *n.* 漆器;漆,天然漆

We put on the second coating of lacquer.

我们上了第二道漆。

5. corrosion [kəˈroʊʒn] *n.* 腐蚀;侵蚀

Look for signs of corrosion.

寻找腐蚀的痕迹。

6. scald [skɔːld] *v.* 烫伤;白灼;*n.* 烧烫伤;沸水

I tried to sip the tea but it was scalding.

我想抿一口茶,可是茶太烫了。

7. implement [ˈɪmpləmənt] *n.* 工具,器械;家具;手段;[法]履行(契约等)

This new implement is a product of the drive for technical innovation.

这种新工具正是技术革新运动的产儿。

8. utensil [juːˈtensl] *n.* 器具;(家庭)用具

This company sells various kinds of kitchen utensils.

这家公司销售各种厨房器具。

9. enamel [ɪˈnæməl] *n.* 搪瓷;珐琅;指甲油

He relied on translucent enamels to produce vivid, glowing pictures.

他利用半透明瓷漆绘制出鲜艳生动的图画。

10. durable [ˈdʊrəbl] *adj.* 耐用的;持久的

This raincoat is made of very durable material.

这件雨衣是用非常耐用的料子做的。

三句必学 The more you practice, the more fluently you will speak.

1. It is believed to be the best material for tea-brewing and purple clay is uniquely able to store and release the fragrance of tea.

紫砂壶被认为最适合泡茶,因为只有这种粘土能够储存和释放茶叶的香味。

2. Using a glass tea set is the best way to enjoy the tea-brewing process.

玻璃茶具泡茶是欣赏冲泡茶的过程的最佳方式。

3. **Enamel** tea sets are smooth, **durable** and chemically resistant.

搪瓷茶具光滑、耐用、耐化学腐蚀。

一篇必读 The more you read, the more knowledge you will get.

People **attach** great importance to what kind of tea set they use. They believed that the tea set affects the flavor of the tea. Here are the 7 most common tea set types in China.

❖ **Pottery Tea Sets —the Best Tools for Brewing Tea**

Pottery is the earliest material that tea sets were made from in China. It is believed to be the best material for tea-brewing and purple clay is uniquely able to store and release the fragrance of tea. After being used many times, the pot itself can flavor the boiled water, without adding any fresh tea leaves.

❖ **Porcelain Tea Sets—the Most Widely Used Tea Sets**

Undoubtedly, China is famous for **porcelain.** It has a long history of usage and porcelain tea sets are very widespread. It also has a high value of art appreciation.

❖ **Lacquer Tea Sets—the Most Artistical Tea Sets**

Lacquer is a special liquid painted on wood or metal. They are not only resistant to damage from water, high temperatures, and acid **corrosion**, but can also be highly artistic with beautiful hand-painted designs.

❖ **Glass Tea Sets—the Best Way to Enjoy Brewing Tea**

Using a glass tea set is the best way to enjoy the tea-brewing process. Glass is relatively inexpensive and easy to shape. However, they are easily broken and it's easy to **scald** the hands when using them.

❖ **Metal Tea Sets—in Fashion 2,000 Years Ago**

A metal tea set was one of the oldest types of household **implement** in China. At first, people used bronze **utensils** for tea, especially during the Qin and the Han dynasties. Nowadays, people rarely use metal tea sets for brewing tea.

❖ **Enamel Tea Sets—the Most Durable Tea Sets**

An **enamel** tea set is a popular craft item in many countries. Enamel is a material made by fusing powdered glass to a substrate by firing. Enamel tea sets are smooth, **durable** and chemically resistant.

❖ **Wood and Bamboo Tea Sets—the Cheapest Tea Sets**

Wood and bamboo tea sets are healthy and they're economical and practical. Wood and bamboo are the cheapest materials for a tea set. The tea-ware used by poor people in society was usually made from wood and bamboo.

1. Describe each tea set in Chinese and English.

In English	In Chinese
Pottery Tea Sets —the Best Tools for Brewing Tea	
	瓷器茶具 ——最广泛使用的茶具
Lacquer Tea Sets —the Most Artistical Tea Sets	
	玻璃茶具 ——享受冲泡茶的最佳方法
Metal Tea Sets —in Fashion 2,000 Years Ago	
	搪瓷茶具 ——最耐用的茶具
Wood and Bamboo Tea Sets —the Cheapest Tea Sets	

2. Fill in the blanks.

_____ is the earliest material that tea sets were made from in China. It is believed to be the best material for tea-brewing and purple clay is uniquely able to store and _____ the fragrance of tea. After being used many times, the pot itself can flavor the _____ water, without adding any fresh tea leaves.

Using a _____ tea set is the best way to enjoy the tea-brewing process. Glass is relatively inexpensive and easy to shape. However, they are easily _____ and it's easy to _____ the hands when using them.

3. Complete your group's speech draft.

Topic: The Most Common Tea Sets in China

🔊 轻松一刻 **The more you share, the happier you will be.**

Chinese Teaism

The chadao integrates the **philosophy**（哲学）, **ethics**（伦理）, the **morals**（道德）in the tea matter activity. Drinking tea can help people mold the character, cultivate the morality, taste the life and grasp the truth, and achieve in the spiritual enjoyment.

"Being harmonious" is the core philosophy of Chinese teaism.

"Being calm" is the key to achieving in Chinese teaism.

"Being joy" is the enjoyment of Chinese tea makers.

"Being real" is the ultimate pursues of Chinese teaism.